MODELING
NARROW-GAUGE RAILROADS

MODELING
NARROW-GAUGE
RAILROADS

BRICK PRICE

CHILTON BOOK COMPANY RADNOR, PENNSYLVANIA

Copyright © 1984 by Brick Price
All Rights Reserved
Published in Radnor, Pennsylvania 19089, by Chilton Book Company
Designed by William E. Lickfield
Manufactured in the United States of America

Library of Congress Cataloging in Publication Data
    Price, Brick.
    Modeling narrow-gauge railroads.
    Bibliography: p. 245
    Includes index.
    1. Railroads—Models. 2. Railroads, Narrow-gauge.
    I. Title.
    TF197.P75 1984   625.1′9   83-43301
    ISBN 0-8019-7293-0 (pbk.)

The Chilton Hobby Series

2 3 4 5 6 7 8 9 0   3 2 1 0 9 8 7 6 5

To my father and mother, who got me going.
To Laura and Eamonn, who keep me going.

ACKNOWLEDGMENTS
My thanks to the staff of Brick Price's Movie Miniatures, especially Darryl Anka, Dale Doane, Noah Dudley, Troy Hughes and Brenda Remhild. I am also indebted to the *Narrow Gauge Gazette* and to *Model Railroader* as sources of constant inspiration, and to Fred Hill of Empire Pacific for feeding my habit with goodies from the Far East.

Contents

MODELING
NARROW-GAUGE RAILROADS

Model Railroading

Model railroading is a fascinating hobby because of the variety of skills the model railroader needs to make realistic models, including electronics, carpentry, painting, photography, and, of course, modeling. Part of the fun of model-railroad building is to meet and beat the many challenges that crop up during the construction of the layout. Most of the procedures outlined in this book are as simple to follow as a cookbook recipe. If you follow the instructions and don't try to shortcut any of the procedures, you should have excellent results the first time through. As your skills develop, you can find new and easier ways to do things.

One of the most rewarding aspects of model railroading is weathering. Part of the joy of viewing real trains is noting the rich textures of heavily aged wood, rusty metal, weather-beaten paint, and soot. You can almost tell the history of a train by the scars it bears. I can sympathize with someone who has spent hundreds of hours building a gorgeous model when it comes time deliberately to tarnish the finish: it's a bit like taking a hammer to a new car. But the model isn't complete until it looks as though it has traveled thousands of miles through all sorts of weather. The sections in this book on super-detailing and weathering describe all the techniques you'll need to create outstanding models.

The information in this book is the result of the combined knowledge of modelers who work for me at Brick Price Movie Miniatures and several club members. Some of the procedures are totally new to this book because we have developed them to cope with the pressures of having to build high-quality, realistic models given little time or money. One of the pri-

Fig. 1-1 It is easy to see from the weathering that this locomotive has seen hard use.

Fig. 1-2 The rail bus is a good example of the kinds of improvised equipment used by the narrow-gauge railroads.

mary considerations we always must face is that the ultimate goal is for the model to appear absolutely real on film. If we fail in that, the illusion of reality in the rest of the film may be lost. Perhaps it's this training and background that makes me appreciate the weathering process.

I've been building models professionally for more than twenty years, and I continue to discover or develop new ideas daily. Every new job brings with it a new set of problems to be solved. The ideas become a part of our repertoire. I also find that I can learn from people who work for me even though they may be relatively new to the business. The point here is, don't assume that you know everything. Many parts of this book may seem elementary if you are experienced, but parts of it will seem brand new. Keep an open mind to learning and you'll be rewarded with exceptional models to display and enjoy.

Once you've established a working layout and some basic skills, you may want to advance to kitbashing or even scratchbuilding. Kitbashing (combining parts from different kits) is an interesting area because it allows you to build complicated-looking models from inexpensive kits where you might otherwise have to scratchbuild the same thing. Included are several

Fig. 1-3 This unusual-looking engine, called a Mason Bogie, was used by many different narrow-gauge railroads.

kitbashed examples, including a how-to section showing the creation of an HOn30 locomotive using an N-scale chassis.

TYPES OF TRAINS

Narrow-gauge railroading is particularly interesting because of its unique rolling stock, equipment, and buildings and the terrain it travels through. To many model railroaders, narrow gauge epitomizes railroading because the trains have so much character. Operations such as logging and mining, foundries, plantations, and sugar trains all use small, interesting equipment. Because most narrow-gauge lines were always financially on the brink of disaster, they had to make do with inferior equipment and work in areas virtually inaccessible by any means other than the railroad. For example, the Denver & Rio Grande Western literally clings to the walls of sheer cliffs for much of its route. The one piece of equipment that most model builders are familiar with is the Galloping Goose, which was made

Fig. 1-4 One of the most appealing aspects of narrow gauge is the array of interesting equipment. This Mason Bogie is an old brass import from the 1960s. I am in the process of restoring it.

from the remains of an old car with a tin box section. This homemade piece of equipment could carry passengers and freight cheaply.

The Denver & South Park was another Colorado-based narrow-gauge line. The D&SP linked up with the D&RGW and yet had a distinctive character of its own, with unusual locomotives and rolling stock. The most familiar locomotive is the Mason Bogie, which has been modeled numerous times by various companies. On this locomotive, the water tank rides over a single truck attached to the train's main frame. Either of these lines is fascinating to model because of the unusual scenery and rolling stock. Virtually every piece of equipment used by these two railroads is available in model form. However, some modelers may want to work with more obscure lines or come up with their own original designs.

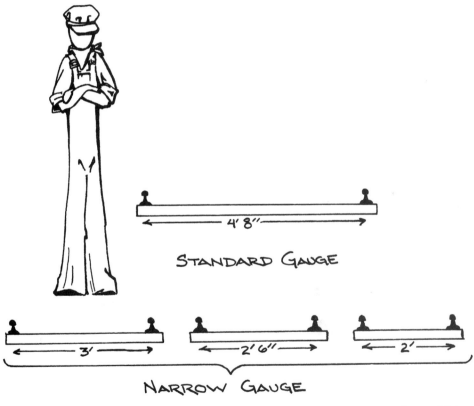

Fig. 1-5 The prospective model railroader has a number of different gauges from which to choose.

CHOOSING A SCALE

The choice of scale is not as obvious today as it was thirty years ago. So many companies produce good-quality, nicely detailed models that the choice of scale becomes one of personal preference and space. Each scale has its own advantages.

All scales have a variety of gauges. The gauge is the width between tracks. We are interested only in narrow gauge or short lines, those gauges less than the standard four feet eight and a half inches. The most popular is three-foot gauge because the first imports were patterned after lines such as the Denver & Rio Grande and Denver & South Park. As time went on, other railroads came to be well known, such as the Sandy River & Rangeley Lakes line, which is a two-foot-gauge line. Depending upon the application, there are gauges as small as eighteen inches and as broad as three and a half feet. The smaller gauge is used for mining and usually includes push carts and electric locomotives.

Fig. 1-6 Placing an HO-scale locomotive next to its 0-scale counterpart readily shows the difference between the two scales.

The larger scales are better for modeling because the detail you add stands out well. It is also easier to build smooth-running locomotives because of the weight. The biggest disadvantage is the amount of room required to build a decent layout, and larger scales cost considerably more to build because of this extra detail. Conversely, the smallest scale, N narrow gauge, is expensive because the chassis used are Z scale; these are expensive because of the intricate engineering required to make such a small functioning locomotive. A happy compromise would seem to be HO narrow gauge. This is the most popular, which means there are more kits available at reasonable prices. The scale is large enough to allow for ample detail and smooth-running equipment. It also allows you to scratchbuild smaller-gauge locomotives, such as two-foot gauge, using N-scale locomotive chassis.

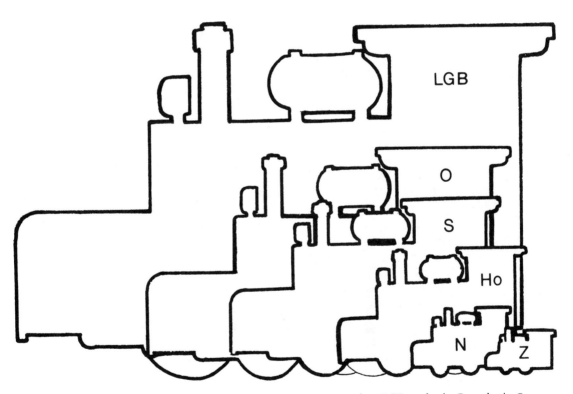

Fig. 1-7 The same train in the different narrow-gauge scales: LGB scale $\frac{1}{32}$, O scale $\frac{1}{48}$, S scale $\frac{1}{64}$, HO scale $\frac{1}{87}$, N scale $\frac{1}{160}$, Z scale $\frac{1}{220}$.

THE ADVANTAGES OF NARROW GAUGE

The most obvious advantage of narrow gauge is the smaller amount of space required to build a decent layout. An 0–4–0T Porter sugar cane plantation locomotive takes up one-tenth of the linear space of a Union Pacific Big Boy and requires a much smaller track radius. An entire train can be modeled in less space than it would take for an A–B–A hookup of a Santa Fe streamliner. Narrow gauge also typically operates in confined areas that would limit the use of bigger trains.

The scenery potential for most narrow-gauge railroads is nearly limitless. The buildings are worn down, the track is unkempt, the locomotives

Fig. 1-8 This narrow-gauge train is dwarfed by its full-sized companion. Courtesy of John T. Derr Collection.

Fig. 1-9 This entire narrow-gauge *consist* (the railroad's term for the makeup of the train) requires less space than the Santa Fe A-B hookup behind it.

are just one side of being derelict, and the people who operate them are usually colorful characters. The nonrailroader would refer to these trains as cute, but we prefer to say that they have character and a railroady flavor. When I was designing the locomotive kits for our Movie Miniatures line, I tried to capture as much of this flavor as possible by combining the best traits of many different types of locomotives, which is a good advantage because it allows you a lot of freedom to express yourself creatively. The real railroads built most of their own equipment from whatever was at hand and made do with whatever they could afford or find. So who is to say that you've made a mistake by combining parts from two different locomotives when the real railroad would have done the same to keep one from the graveyard?

A smaller railroad is much easier to design because the prototypes

Fig. 1-10 While not an exact replica of any one engine, this Movie Miniature's kit has the feel of the old narrow-gauge engines.

had steeper grades than did their standard-gauge contemporaries. Also, many narrow gauge or short lines were so short that the entire railroad comprised no more than two miles of track. Therefore, it would be possible to model the entire railroad in the average home. Try that with the Santa Fe!

Research: Sources of Information

The research necessary to create truly realistic models can add to the enjoyment of model railroading. Every modeler, from the beginner to the professional, should work from reference photographs of the real railroad he wants to re-create. Hundreds of publications are available on obscure narrow-gauge lines, and some of the more popular lines have whole books devoted to them. One source of information that even professional modelers tend to overlook is the local library, where there are hundreds of illustrated books and large dictionaries and encyclopedias that contain several pages of color plates on the more common locomotives and rolling stock. (See the Bibliography at the back of the book for a list of reference books on narrow-gauge railroads.)

MODEL RAILROADING CLUBS

Joining a model-railroading club can increase your knowledge of the hobby fairly quickly. Clubs provide a number of benefits to their members, including monthly bulletins and regular meetings where you can get help with modeling problems. Clubs will often pool the skills and resources of all their members to create a large, sophisticated layout that would be far beyond the resources of one person.

HISTORICAL SOCIETIES

Historical societies provide a clearinghouse of information for the model railroader. Each society specializes in a particular type of railroad and publishes newsletters and magazines devoted to its particular trains.

Fig. 2-1 A symbiotic relationship where everyone profits: the Narrow Gauge Guild has an inexpensive area to house a layout (not to mention an unlimited stock of spare parts), and the Whistle Stop in Pasadena has a display layout to show equipment in operation and how construction is done.

Most of the members in these societies are modelers. There is usually a membership fee to enroll in a historical society, but it is well worth it. In addition to newsletters and magazines, they often give advance notice of forthcoming books and other publications.

RAILROADING CATALOGS, MAGAZINES, AND BOOKS

Model railroad equipment catalogs are an essential part of your library. There is a catalog available for every scale of train, and each is filled with pictures and descriptions of products available.

Railroading magazines devoted to both real railroads and miniature ones are invaluable. They include informative articles on types of trains and how to model them, advertisements on new products, a calendar of shows and events, club information, and model railroad stores. There are even a few magazines available devoted entirely to narrow-gauge railroading, such as the *Narrow Gauge and Short Line Gazette*.

There are hundreds of books available on model trains, including

Fig. 2-2 A train museum can be a treasure trove of information for a modeler.

Robert Schleicher's three-volume set of books in Chilton's "Model Railroading Handbook" series. These books provide complete information on the planning, building, and operation of model trains.

FIELD TRIPS

Whenever you have an opportunity to observe an actual narrow-gauge railroad in operation, take it. Although books and model-railroading clubs are invaluable resources for the modeler, they can't replace the experience of actually seeing the trains that you are re-creating. Most large cities have train museums where you can see (and often even climb on) many of the older trains that were used locally. Almost every state has at least one narrow-gauge railroad in operation, and a visit will yield a wealth of information about operating procedures, track types and size, train details, and other important data. And it's much more fun than sitting in a cloistered library rummaging through books on a sunny summer day.

One thing to remember when you're viewing a real train is the years of weatherbeating it has seen. Try to imagine what the structures looked

Fig. 2-3 It is well worth the effort to find a narrow-gauge railroad that is still operating. The Yosemite Mountain–Sugar Pine Railroad hauls tourists in Yosemite National Park. The engine was built in 1928; railroad has the largest narrow-gauge shay ever built. Photo by Joseph Bispo; courtesy of Yosemite Mountain–Sugar Pine Railroad.

like when they were new and well maintained. No one sets out deliberately to build old-looking trains or buildings, except perhaps for an amusement park, but I prefer to make most of my scenery and rolling stock look as though it's on its last legs just prior to the line going bankrupt. If it's not dirty and beat up, it's no good.

If you're lucky, you may be able to travel close to home on a field trip and spend little more than a day. If you live in Maine, however, you could travel for several weekends without covering the same ground twice. Otherwise, you may want to plan a vacation around a trip to one of the more famous lines. I wonder how many people have made the pilgrimage to Colorado to see the Galloping Geese.

Fig. 2-4 Amusement parks are also a source for research material for modeling. For example, Knott's Berry Farm has restored to operating condition this original Denver & Rio Grande Southern equipment. Photo courtesy of Knott's Berry Farm.

Elsewhere in this book, I've included a list of the better operating narrow-gauge and short-line railroads of interest. Don't discount amusement parks for research either. Many parts of Disneyland's railroad were designed by Ward Kimball, Walt Disney, and John Olson, all avid train buffs. The Disneyland locomotives once hauled freight and passengers for real. The diminutive Porter-style locomotives at Knott's Berry Farm have been converted to electricity from steam, but they still have most of their original appointments. Much of Knott's amusement railroad, in fact, is made from restored D&RGW equipment.

THE CAMERA AS A SCALING TOOL

A camera is one of the best modeling aids you can have. It can be used not only to record information, but to provide accurate scaling. A properly shot photo in the hands of one of our modelers is as good as or better than a set of blueprints. Most people tend to shoot a building or other object to be modeled so that it looks attractive or dramatic. This is OK, but it's usually at odds with what you will need to re-create the scene

15

Fig. 2-5 Putting a person in your photograph will help you to get an idea of the relative sizes of objects.

for your layout. Instead, shoot from a low, three-quarter angle (with your camera at eye level or lower) from several points around the building. This will show off form and color. Be sure to include a scale reference. I use a pair of sticks with alternating black-and-white foot-long stripes. These stripes show up well against any backdrop and are always in scale to the object being photographed. Shoot all pictures from the same distance to the object, and be sure that the lab prints them full frame to avoid scaling differences from one picture to the next. If you don't have a scale handy, try to include a person in the picture. You can later create a scale ruler to measure details. A six-foot-tall person is ideal because the increments can be easily divided.

Next, shoot views of the object at right angles to all planes (keep the camera level) to eliminate perspective as much as possible. Any object will require a minimum of four such shots. It would be nice to get a shot looking down on the object, but this is usually impossible. When you're done, you should have a minimum of eight shots of the object. We usually take an entire roll of pictures from every angle and of every part to create our movie models, and sometimes even that is not enough.

When you start building the model, the value of the photos will become obvious. If your pictures are the same relative size, make up a scale ruler based on the scale reference in the picture. If you're careful when shooting, or if you can print the pictures to scale, you may be able to use an existing scale ruler.

All is not lost if you don't have a convenient reference in the picture. Any single measurement can be used. A door opening is usually about six and a half feet high and is the single most standard item. You can usually guess at one dimension. For instance, a locomotive doesn't always have a door, but you know that the roof has to be at least a foot or 18 inches above the engineer's head. Try to obtain one dimension for later reference.

All bets are off if your only reference is a single perspective photo. You might be able to determine the height at a given point, but that will change. All dimensions will diminish as the object recedes into the background. I'm sure there is some clever way of solving this problem, but I've always had to rely on intuitive deduction and pray that it works out. So far I've been fairly lucky.

Prototype Railroad Lines

Now that you have chosen a scale for your layout, you will need to make some basic decision about how it will look. One of the first decisions is the kind of railroad you want to create. Will it be a Rocky Mountain line that carries passengers and freight through steep mountain passes, or will it be a sugar plantation train that hauls sugar cane through the jungle? The possibilities are as boundless as your imagination. To help you in your decision making, here is a summary of some of the more popular narrow-gauge lines.

DENVER & RIO GRANDE WESTERN

Probably the best-known narrow-gauge line in the United States, the D&RGW serves the mines in the Rockies, hauling ore through some of the most spectacular scenery in the country. Because it is so well known, especially the "Galloping Goose" rail cars, many commercial kits exist. There is also an excellent historical society, the Colorado Railroad Historical Foundation, which is willing to help modelers with their research.

DENVER & SOUTH PARK

Another famous Rocky Mountain line, the D&SP, began operations in 1874 and ran various routes until 1936. Badly managed, badly laid out, and poorly financed, it teetered on the brink of financial ruin for most of its existence. For this reason, it, even more than other narrow-gauge railroads, is known for its peculiar, improvised equipment. The Mason Bogie

Fig. 3-1 The Durango & Silverton line pictured here hauled freight and passengers through the Rockies. The Denver & Rio Grande Western, the Denver & South Park, and the Uintah were also well-known railways. (Photo courtesy of Durango & Silverton Railroad)

style locomotive (see Figure 1-4) originated with this line, and a few examples run to this day.

UINTAH RAILWAY

Built in 1904, the Uintah was one of the last narrow-gauge railways to be built in Colorado. It was built to haul Gilsonite out of the Uintah Valley in northeastern Colorado, and its trains traveled along some of the steepest grades in the Rockies. The Uintah used articulated Mallets (mal'let) built especially for them by the Baldwin Locomotive Works because of the steep grades and sharp curves. Surrounded by impressive scenery and

Fig. 3-2 The Sandy River & Rangeley Lakes Railroad used engines like this one to haul cranberries through the woods of Maine.

funky equipment, it is a prototypical narrow-gauge railway at its very best and its very worst.

SANDY RIVER & RANGELEY LAKES

Built in 1849 and still operating to a limited extent today, the Sandy River & Rangeley Lakes line uses a two-foot-gauge track, making it the smallest railroad gauge in use in the United States. It was used mostly to haul lumber, cranberries, and maple syrup through the woods of Maine.

NACIÓNALES DE MEXICO

Alive and well today, the Naciónales de Mexico is a nationally owned line that uses cast-off American three-foot-gauge motive power and equipment. To ride this line is like stepping back fifty years in railroading history! Nowhere else in the world can you see so many Baldwin locomotives still running. This line would be a natural for someone wanting

Fig. 3-3 A typical car used in Hawaii to carry sugar cane.

Fig. 3-4 Narrow-gauge trains served both sides with distinction during both world wars. Photo courtesy of National Archives.

Fig. 3-5 This narrow-gauge locomotive is a good example of the trench trains used during World War I. Photo courtesy of National Archives.

to model a contemporary line while retaining a natural mix of steam and diesel power.

SUGAR AND COTTON PLANTATION TRAINS

The scattered sugar plantations on the Hawaiian Islands needed some way to transport laborers and goods to and from the docks. The narrow-gauge railways served these needs perfectly. Porter locomotives were popular here, but a great deal of Japanese equipment was used, such as Kato or Kroso steam locomotives. Almost all of Hawaii's extensive narrow-gauge systems were wiped out in a hurricane and tidal wave shortly after World War II, but while they were operating, the sugar trains ran through some of the lushest scenery in the world.

Because their needs were similar, cotton plantations in the American

Fig. 3-6 One form of narrow-gauge railroading that is almost completely ignored is intra-urban transportation such as this San Francisco cable car.

South used trains that were similar to sugar plantation trains, but without the Japanese equipment. However, a few companies did use European power.

MILITARY TRAINS

Often referred to as "trench trains," narrow-gauge trains were used by the French and German forces during both world wars to move artillery, troops, and supplies. The Germans, in fact, used their narrow-gauge equipment in South Africa and even sent twenty-one narrow-gauge locomotives to China with the troops that suppressed the Boxer Rebellion. That would be an intriguing and unusual situation for a diorama! Surprisingly, many of the smaller trains used in the United States during the war were of foreign manufacture. It wouldn't be uncommon to see a French 0-6-OT shuttling tanks at dockside in New York.

It is also possible to model a picturesque European village with American trains and military miniatures. This is an excellent excuse for a train buff to get into military equipment for awhile and produce some unique dioramas. For more information about the interesting sidelights in railroading history, see Charles S. Small's book *Two-Foot Rails to the Front*.

Tools and the Workshop

Tools are essential for model building whether you construct kits or build from scratch. The most important thing you could ever do as a modeler is to buy good-quality tools and learn how to use them properly. A simple tool kit can be put together for less than ten dollars and should consist of a modeler's knife, a half-round file, sandpaper, glue, and bottled paints. From this simple beginning, the avid modeler or professional can literally spend thousands of dollars.

SOLDERING

Soldering is an essential skill for modeling trains. It's needed for wiring and brass-locomotive assembly or modification. Too often beginning modelers shy away from soldering simply because they're afraid of the unknown. But it is the only satisfactory method of joining brass parts, and the techniques are simple. If you've never tried soldering before, practice on a piece of scrap first until you've learned the technique.

You should get a small soldering pencil, a large soldering iron, a small acetylene torch, and a soldering gun. A soldering pencil is good for tiny pieces and for wiring or wood burning. The large iron will yield enough heat for joining sheets of brass or brass turnings such as smokestacks. The soldering gun is a convenience item because it heats up quickly and has a fairly small tip.

Soldering with a torch is quicker and simpler than with an iron because the area to be joined is heated quickly. This rapid heating also means that there is less chance for adjacent parts to be loosened as heat is trans-

24

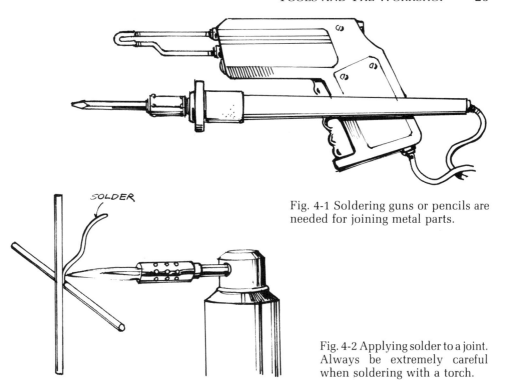

Fig. 4-1 Soldering guns or pencils are needed for joining metal parts.

SOLDER

Fig. 4-2 Applying solder to a joint. Always be extremely careful when soldering with a torch.

ferred. Exercise extreme caution at all times when using or storing a torch and tanks. Small tanks, available from surgical supply houses, will meet most of your needs. If you're using large tanks, chain them in place so they don't topple over and check the valves for leaks by brushing soapy water over the joints.

Note: Acetylene can "pool" in areas and cause serious damage if ignited. Wear goggles at all times, and be sure to turn the oxygen on last and off first to avoid an explosion.

LAYOUT AND DESIGN

Every modeling job requires some planning and design. Even a simple, straight saw cut must be defined or the tool can wander and ruin the job. The most basic layout tool is a 6-inch flexible steel ruler about $\frac{1}{2}$ inch wide, graduated to $\frac{1}{32}$ inch on one edge and $\frac{1}{64}$ inch on the other, with tenths and millimeters on the back side. You will probably want a ruler for whatever scale model you're building. Then you can make direct measurements

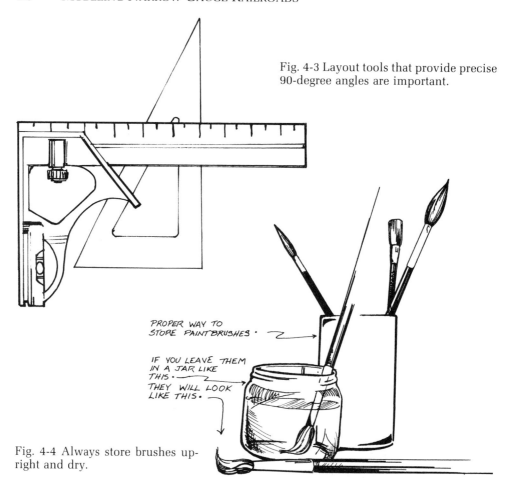

Fig. 4-3 Layout tools that provide precise 90-degree angles are important.

PROPER WAY TO
STORE PAINTBRUSHES.

IF YOU LEAVE THEM
IN A JAR LIKE
THIS.
THEY WILL LOOK
LIKE THIS.

Fig. 4-4 Always store brushes upright and dry.

from blueprints, which will eliminate the need for confusing calculations. A carpenter's square or a machinist's square is good for making sure that parts are aligned and true. On a train model, this is particularly important.

Considerable time and effort can be saved by using locking dividers to transfer dimensions from drawings to the work piece. You can even double or triple the scale of the drawings easily by stepping off the dimensions (walking the divider legs). Thus $\frac{1}{16}$-scale drawings can be used to model directly a $\frac{1}{48}$-scale object.

A sharp pencil with medium (No. 2) lead is satisfactory for layout work on wood, but a scribe is needed for plastic or metal. Machinist's dye (such as Dyekem or even a blue marker) will make layout work easier on metal or plastic. The center of holes to be drilled first must be located with a center punch or the drill will wander. The depression of a punch mark keeps the drill exactly on center.

Most art supply stores have an excellent selection of templates, ranging from simple triangles to french curves and eclipse templates. Most templates are inexpensive, and you'll probably want several. A hole template is also handy for measuring the diameters of dowel, but be aware that allowances are made for pencil width, so the template hole may be slightly larger than indicated. Never attempt to free-hand a compound curve.

BRUSHES

Watercolor brushes are ideal for model work. A good brush can lay a coat of paint on a model almost as evenly as a spray can, and it will keep a fine point, so it can be used for both broad strokes and fine lettering. Size 3 holds about the right amount of paint for most major model work. For painting larger areas, use a size 5 brush.

Clean brushes thoroughly so that no paint dries near the base of the bristles. Otherwise they will break off later and spoil your work. Use an enamel thinner that is recommended for the paint you're using. The same brush can be used with any kind of paint so long as you clean it thoroughly each time. Careful cleaning will add years to the life of a good brush. Store brushes with the point ends up.

AIRBRUSH AND COMPRESSOR

An airbrush isn't an essential tool for modeling, but it can place your work in the expert category. Everything on a model must be miniaturized to the same scale. A large brush will leave heavy marks and give the scale away instantly. The airbrush is a miniature version of a spray gun and applies a smooth, fine coat of paint.

A good compressor with a large storage tank is handy to power the airbrush, but you can get by with a smaller compressor or even with an aerosol can such as the type sold by Paasche or Binks.

Paasche makes one of the best airbrushes, but a Binks or Thayer-Chandler will also do a good job.

TAPS AND DIES

Many assembly jobs require the use of nuts and bolts and tapping and threading. Tapping is the operation of making threads inside holes. Threading makes external threads on a rod or similar part.

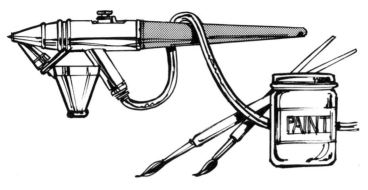

Fig. 4-5 The airbrush gives a professional-looking finish to your model.
Detail painting is done with fine watercolor brushes.

Fig. 4-6 A die (far right) is used to put threads on a
rod, while a tap (near right) is used to put threads
inside a hole.

A useful range of taps includes 00–90, 0–80, 2–56, and 4–40. The first numbers of a reference number (00, 0, 2, 4) indicate the diameter, while the second numbers refer to the number of threads per inch. Taps can be held in a regular tap handle or pin vise.

In addition, for each tap, you'll need a drill. Tables of tap and drill size are available, but it is just as easy to select the drill that will just pass through the hole in a nut of the same size as the tap and use this as the tap drill.

To use a tap, drill the hole with the tap drill and remove any accumulation of chips. Insert the tap, keeping it at right angles to the surface, and begin to turn it very carefully. After several turns, remove the tap and blow or shake the chips out of the hold. Reinsert the tap, make several more turns, and again remove it. Continue to do this until the hole is fully threaded. Like most cutting tools, a tap is brittle and the slightest excess pressure will break it, so proceed cautiously and never apply too much torque to the tap wrench or pin vise.

Threading is performed with threading dies held in a die holder. It is accomplished much the same as tapping, except that you are working on a rod, tubing, or square stock filed down to approximate size. The end of the piece to be threaded must be tapered slightly to give the die a chance to grip. Use lubricants when tapping or threading to prevent binding. When tapping or threading plastic, special care must be taken to avoid heating the work, since the tap or die will seize. It's best to use soap as a lubricant or work under running water.

POWER TOOLS

The one power tool most valuable to the modeler is the type manufactured by such companies as Dremel, Foredom, and Casco. These tools are extremely versatile, and attachments such as saws, burrs, grinding tools, and even miniature sanding drums are available. They operate at high speeds and will cut, sand, or grind rapidly. The overall dimension of the tool is small, permitting inside cuts and finishing operations with ease.

JEWELER'S LATHE

A lathe is a worthwhile addition to any workshop, but it can be an expensive one. The least expensive lathe available, the German-made Unimat, costs around $300. American-made metal-working lathes start at $350. A small economy lathe can be purchased at Sears and Roebuck, but after adding the cost of accessories, you might as well buy the Unimat.

SAFETY EQUIPMENT

Always try to keep your work area clean and neat. Put tools away when you are not using them, especially small, sharp tools, since they are

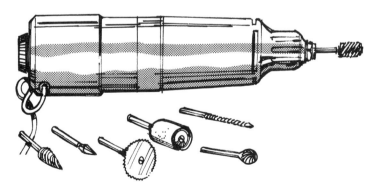

Fig. 4-7 Power hand tools can be used for cutting, grinding, shaping, sanding, and polishing.

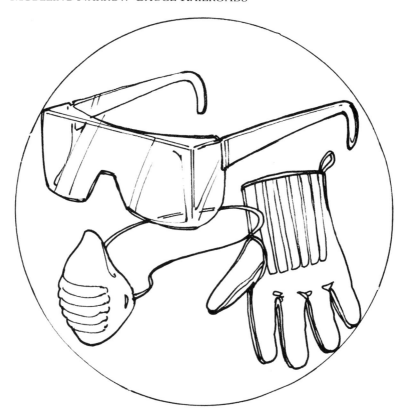

Fig. 4-8 Always use the appropriate protective gear when working with toxic materials or power tools.

easily lost in piles of junk and can cause serious injuries. Many a modeler has nearly lost a finger to a sharp X-Acto knife.

Be careful when working with adhesives and paints. Some are toxic and can cause serious damage if inhaled. Lacquer paints contain solvents that also are hazardous. Work in a well-ventilated area unless the product is clearly labeled as being nontoxic.

Always wear safety glasses when using power tools. Small pieces of wood and chips of styrene can be as painful and dangerous as metal shavings. Take good care of your eyes. If you should get any type of glue, solvent, or paint in your eye, call a physician immediately and rinse the eye with cool, clear water for at least five minutes. Do not rub the eye with your fingers.

Some materials can be extremely volatile and explosive. Even sawdust can be as explosive as gasoline with the right mixture of air and dust. And it takes only one spark to level a house.

Lighting is also important for proper vision and safety. Use a drafting fluorescent desk light or industrial lamp for even lighting.

Always keep clear of power tools and never wear loose clothing or jewelry while working.

THE WORKBENCH

A permanent home for your tools and projects is just as important as any of the tools or techniques described in this book. A workbench can make your hobby much more enjoyable and efficient and give you a comfortable, organized work area. For details regarding construction of a simple workbench, see *The Model-Building Handbook* by Brick Price (also published by Chilton).

STORAGE

The most useful modeling tool since the X-Acto knife is a plastic-bag sealer. The ideas and applications are endless. A plastic-bag sealer is a relatively new kitchen-aid device that can completely heat-seal a plastic bag. The bag is then impervious to air and outside moisture. Most of the common types are made for only one brand of bag (the manufacturer's, of course) and have limited usefulness. General Electric's "Bag Sealer" will seal any plastic bag, so this is the model to buy.

The GE unit is simple to use, but you may want to practice a little before tackling a prize job. Place the open end of the bag over the wire under the lid. Smooth out any wrinkles and air bubbles toward the opening. Make the seal as close to the object as possible. This will prevent waste and allow less moisture to accumulate. Never seal a moist item that can rot or rust. A little moisture in a prized catalog or on a precision tool can be disastrous. Metal items should be given a coat of WD-40 or gun oil prior to sealing. You'll be amazed at how fresh everything will stay over the years. This process is better than mummification.

Plastic bags available in grocery stores are expensive, so first try war surplus or hardware stores, which sell bags in hundred lots in various sizes at approximately a penny a bag. This is the most economical way to go. Grocery store bags are useful, though, since they are thicker, and some can be frozen or boiled. I use freezer bags for storing film and Krazy Glue. They can also be used for heating paint in the bottle while minimizing

Fig. 4-9 A kitchen bag sealer is valuable for storing parts, kits, or even complete locomotives such as this one.

the risk of the bottle breaking. *Caution:* Do not place paints, glues, thinners, or other flammable substances in boiling water. Turn off the flame and leave it off while warming these substances.

Here is a small sample of the bag sealer's usefulness:

- To store books, model catalogs, magazines, and instruction sheets.
- To store die-cast parts to prevent rusting and paint deterioration. This also keeps rubber parts from hardening so quickly.
- To keep mixed bottles of paints, or to extend the shelf life of glues, paints, and batteries through refrigeration.
- To separate parts during a complicated or critical assembly. Subassemblies can be kept clean, dry, and safe.

- To bag and price items for sale at a swap meet. You'll never lose the price and information about the model if you bag it at home first. This also keeps models from being scratched or damaged in transit.
- To consolidate kits. Many parts of kits are hard to throw away, but kits can soon take over a whole house. I bag the kit parts with the instruction sheet and put the bags in a large box for easy storage or hang them from the rafters with nails or wire.

PROTECTING MODEL PARTS

Whenever I buy a new kit, I place the chrome parts in a bag and seal it immediately. I do this because these parts usually get scratched or discolor before I get around to building the model. Most manufacturers bag the unplated plastic parts, which doesn't make a bit of sense.

There are many handy, expensive tools that are invaluable when needed

Fig. 4-10 For modelers who are more interested in building trains than in running them, a display case is a good way to show off your models and protect them.

but that often go unused for months, such as a small spare saw or knife blades. A quick spray with WD-40 will protect them.

Anyone who lives in Los Angeles knows about rubber rotting from ozone exposure. Smog, heat, and moisture can ruin rubber in no time. Coat rubber parts with silicone or WD-40 prior to bagging. You can even restore badly hardened rubber by soaking it in Armor-All or silicone while sealed.

5

Modeling Materials

Materials are an important consideration for any project, since your choice of material at the beginning of a job can ultimately affect the model's finished appearance. It can also determine how you feel about the model as work progresses. A poor choice of material, or a cheap material, can make your work difficult and tedious. Cheap products can even add to the cost of the finished model, since you may have to redo much of the work. A good example of this would be to use balsa wood for a building rather than good bass wood. The balsa will fuzz and splinter while you're working with it and will require additional sealing when finished. The model will feel lighter and lose that good-quality heft. If that isn't enough, the texture and grain will be grossly out of scale. It isn't worth the savings of a few pennies now to have an inferior model later.

The sections in this chapter will list the best building materials and the adhesives to use with them. It won't do any good to use good materials unless you can stick them all together in the end.

WOODS

Wood is the best choice for the traditional model builder to use for buildings and old-fashioned rolling stock. The best types are bass, clear pine, jelutong, and walnut. These woods have a very fine grain and all are relatively hard. The woods you'll need will vary with the application. Some woods are chosen for their carving characteristics. Gelutung is an excellent wood for carving. Clear pine and bass are perfect for planking, spindle turning, or general construction. Walnut is best for a display base.

Fig. 5-1 Buildings are available in a variety of materials. This inexpensive station is a Woodland Scenics metal kit that is loaded with detail.

Each of the construction chapters will tell you what is best to use for a given application.

PLASTICS

Styrene is the plastic used by most kit manufacturers because of its low cost and its ability to reproduce fine detail. The best type is a virgin white styrene, which is pliable and easy to shape and glue. Clear styrene is brittle, crazes easily, and will shatter like glass if you try to score and snap it like other plastics. Pigments generally weaken styrene and change its characteristics. Black, for instance, has a high degree of carbon, making

Fig. 5-2 Here is an interesting concept. This FM Minitrix diesel has a solid brass body. I had the stock plastic body burned out in brass as the beginning of a conversion. The model came through with perfect detail and at only $10. The model now has substantially more weight for added traction and all pieces can be soldered together for a durable model.

it soft and gummy. Be careful when gluing any pigmented plastic. Evergreen produces a line of styrene strips in scale lumber sizes.

Fiberglass and resin both require mixing chemicals to create hard parts. Resin, either polyester or epoxy, can be used for molding parts. There are new polyurethanes on the market that can reproduce parts from molds with less hassle, but these are generally available only in gallon cans, which are too expensive for home use.

METALS

Many modelers prefer the look and feel of metal parts on their models. Different types of metals are appropriate for different uses. Here is a guide to the various metals commonly used in modeling.

Brass

Brass can be readily machined and soldered together to form model parts of beauty and substance. Most commercially available parts are made either of brass or white metal. Be sure to use solder that is intended for brass. Silver-bearing solder is strong, but it requires a lot of heat for bonding. A low-temperature solder such as Tix is best for most applications.

Fig. 5-3 This tiny HOn30 locomotive is built entirely of brass. It is expensive, but its value will appreciate over the years.

Aluminum

Aluminum is easy to work with and can be polished to resemble silver, but it can't be welded or soldered easily. In fact, most glues and paints don't work well on it either. If you must make something from aluminum, fasten the pieces together with screws.

Steel

Steel has limited applications for model railroading, except for making brackets or mounts. Although it can be silver-soldered or welded, it is better to use brass.

ADHESIVES

No one adhesive is suitable for all of the assembly jobs that crop up in the construction of a model. Here are some of the adhesives that are available.

Acetate Cement

Common acetate-type cements are Ambroid, Duco, and other "model airplane" or "household" cements. Most of them are fast drying. Acetate cement is made by dissolving celluloid in acetone. Most formulations contain additional ingredients to promote strength and fast drying. I rarely use these glues because of their odor and weak bonding, but you may find them ideal. Use these adhesives only on wood or on the few older acetate-plastic kits that are still available. They are not satisfactory for metal or styrene plastic.

Good results are obtained by applying the cement to one of the parts to be joined, adding the other part, and letting the assembly dry. Better joints can sometimes be obtained on porous surfaces if a thin coat is applied to one part just before assembly.

Plastic Cement

Plastic cements are available in several consistencies, ranging from that of syrup to water. The latter, sold in glass jars with an applicator brush, are specifically made for styrene and are not suitable for other uses.

The biggest problem with styrene cement results from using too much, since the softened plastic will ooze out of the joint onto adjoining surfaces. Apply a thin coat to each surface to be joined, let it dry slightly, then join the parts. Save all scraps of plastic and put them into a small container filled with acetone. For safety's sake, be sure the container has a tight-fitting cover. Acetone doesn't dissolve plastic completely, but after about forty-eight hours it will have softened the plastic to a puttylike consistency that makes an excellent filler. It will dry in a minute or so, depending on how thickly it's applied. With a small knife, it can be formed to any shape while still soft. This putty will be useful for filling unsightly gaps and joint lines on plastic models.

Use EDC (ethylene dichloride) for joining Lucite, Plexiglas, or other acrylic plastics. This is a watery liquid and is easily applied to a joint while the parts are held together. Capillary action makes the liquid flow into the seam. This cement does not seem to etch acrylics, so you don't have to be as careful when applying it. Plastruct makes a blend of this liquid, called Weld-On, which is used for bonding ABS plastics.

White Glue

White resin-emulsion adhesive is sold under the trade names "Elmer's Glue" and "Magic Cement." It is known generically as white glue, and it comes in a polyethylene squeeze bottle with a pinhole spout, which makes it easy to apply. Because white glue becomes transparent when it dries, it is most useful for adding clear parts such as lamp lenses to a finished

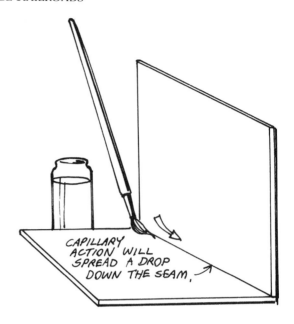

CAPILLARY ACTION WILL SPREAD A DROP DOWN THE SEAM.

Fig. 5-4 The correct way to apply adhesive.

model. It will not etch plastic or damage painted surfaces, and it is water-soluble until it dries. Excess cement can be wiped off with a damp cloth if you work rapidly. Follow the directions on the bottle and apply a thin coat to each surface, clamping until dry. A bond also can be achieved with a single coat and pressureless drying. White glue will dry more slowly than most other glues, but the joint will be very strong. Use white glue primarily for joining wood.

Aliphatic Resin

Aliphatic resin is similar in use and application to white glue. It is yellowish in color and packaged almost identically. This adhesive catalyzes and sets up faster than white glue, but the cleanup is the same.

Contact Cement

Goodyear's "Pliobond" and Walther's "Goo" are typical of resin-type contact cements. The one type of adhesive that can be used for joining metal parts, they are applied to both surfaces to be joined and allowed to dry until tacky. Then the parts can be assembled. These adhesives are messy to use, and their very nature requires that their use be limited to the assembly of flat surfaces. Final hardening may take months.

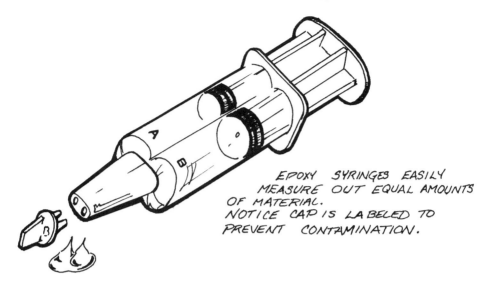

EPOXY SYRINGES EASILY
MEASURE OUT EQUAL AMOUNTS
OF MATERIAL.
NOTICE CAP IS LABELED TO
PREVENT CONTAMINATION.

Fig. 5-5 Epoxy comes in handy dispensers or in tubes. Be careful not to mix the two parts when storing them or they will harden.

Rubber Cement

Rubber cement, similar to contact cement, is normally used in tire repairs and for various office tasks. Its main usefulness to the train modeler is in making temporary bonds, as in attaching patterns to wood or metal. After the parts have been cut out, the patterns can be peeled off and any remaining cement rubbed off.

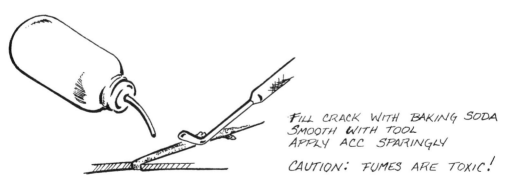

FILL CRACK WITH BAKING SODA
SMOOTH WITH TOOL
APPLY ACC SPARINGLY

CAUTION: FUMES ARE TOXIC!

Fig. 5-6 An exceptionally strong bond can be created and large gaps can be filled using ACC (Hot Stuff, Krazy Glue) and baking soda. Do not inhale the fumes, and be sure to work in a well-ventilated area.

Epoxy

Epoxy is greatly overrated as an adhesive for general use. Epoxy cures rather than drying like a glue and is better suited for bonding nonporous materials such as metal or glass. Epoxies are generally marketed in matching tubes, which are mixed together in a one-to-one ratio. Whenever you work with epoxy, be careful that you don't get any on your skin or in your eyes.

Hot Stuff/Krazy Glue

Hot Stuff and Krazy Glue can be mixed with baking soda to form a hard fillet or to increase the effectiveness of a butt bond. Be sure to avoid inhaling the fumes. If you use caution, these adhesives can become an important part of your modeling.

Trackwork

The first step in building any layout is to devise an overall plan. The type of layout you choose to build will depend on a number of factors, including the type of railroad, the space available and the amount of time you will have to work on it, and, last but not least, your budget. An excellent rule of thumb to follow (particularly if this is your first layout) is to avoid designing a huge, sprawling pike that looks wonderful on paper but is beyond your capabilities to construct. Many layouts are never completed because the modeler tried to do too much too soon and grew discouraged.

You will get far more enjoyment from a moderate-sized layout that is complete and operating than from a behemoth that is never finished. The construction skills you'll learn building the smaller railroad will serve you in good stead if you do decide to build a larger layout later on. In addition, a smaller layout can often be incorporated into a larger design at a later date. One of the largest and most spectacular model railroads ever built, the late John Allen's Gorre & Daphetid Railroad, first saw the light of day as a modest $3\frac{1}{2} \times 6$ foot HO layout. It ultimately became the basis of the much larger, final G&D plan.

The method of modeling you choose will also affect the type of track plan you wind up with. One method, called freelance, is to make up an entirely fictitious railroad and not use a prototype. In freelance design it is entirely up to you to decide on the type of scenery, the style of buildings and the name of the town, what industries the road serves, and the type of rolling stock. Although you have essentially a free license to do anything, maintain some sense of balance in your choices or the ultimate effect of the layout will suffer. No matter how much you may enjoy the sight of a huge articulated Mallet steaming along, no one will buy the idea that it is hauling cranberries through the Maine woods, instead of a tiny Porter.

Another method of design is to model as accurately as possible an actual, or prototypical, railroad. Although obviously limited by space availability, prototype modeling follows actual landscape types, industry, and types of rolling stock used on the actual road. Prototype design is the most challenging method from a strict modeling standpoint, since everything on the layout must be carefully researched for authenticity and then re-created in miniature. A well-researched and constructed prototype layout can be one of the finest examples of model railroading as an art. One disadvantage of this method, however, is that it can be somewhat limiting, since you are restricted to prototype equipment and operations. If you want to haul mine trains and the prototype is strictly a logging operation, you must choose a different prototype.

A more flexible method, and the one most commonly seen in model layout design, is known as combination modeling. As the name implies, this method uses aspects of both freelance and prototype design. In its most common form it usually represents a freelanced smaller railroad operating as a branch or feeder line with connections to a nearby mainline prototype road. This allows the modeler considerable freedom in setting up the equipment, operations, and scenery (which may or may not represent a specific geographical area). This allows the logical use of prototype equipment on a make-believe pike. The type of traffic carried by the prototype can also help determine possible operations on the branch line by suggesting related businesses served by either or both lines and passenger connections to larger towns or cities served by the prototype.

Once you have decided on the type of railroad and the modeling method to use to create it, the next step is to develop a final track plan showing trackwork, scenery types, and possible structure locations. There are a number of collections of published track plans on the market, and the various model railroad magazines usually publish at least one plan per issue. By studying published plans you can familiarize yourself with different types of layouts, gain ideas of features you might want to include in a plan, and perhaps even find a track plan suitable to your needs that can be used without modification. This is more likely with freelanced or combination layouts, since prototype layouts are usually designed to reflect specific sections of country or train operations. However, there are even published plans based on some of the better-known prototype roads.

Don't limit yourself to the first appropriate plan you find. Experiment with different track arrangements and scenery until you find a combination you like. Once you have designed a suitable plan, put it away for a few days and then come back to review it. You may suddenly see additions or changes that were not apparent before. It is far easier to thrash out the final design changes on paper than to make changes in the layout itself after construction is underway.

Once the track plan is finalized, there is one further step to take that will help you further visualize the final layout appearance before beginning the actual construction. Use the final plan as a guide and make a small scale model of what the finished layout will look like. A scale of $\frac{1}{4}$ or $\frac{1}{2}$ inch to the foot is usually sufficient. Use strips of thin cardboard for the tracks, modeling clay for the scenery, and small blocks of balsa or basswood to represent buildings. This may give you still more ideas for modifications of the final design. When you're finally satisfied with the model, keep it nearby as a guide when working on the layout itself.

BENCHWORK

Benchwork refers to the various structures that support the scenery, buildings, and trackwork of the layout. These include the sub-roadbed,

Fig. 6-1 Many modelers prefer to hand-lay track rather than purchase ready-made track sections. Although it provides a realistic track profile and the uneven look of narrow-gauge railroading, it is time misspent.

Fig. 6-2 This track is larger than usual, but it does point out the realism of the spikes, track, and ties.

which actually supports the track; the framework that supports the sub-roadbed and is the base on which much of the scenery rests; and the mounting brackets or legs, which support the whole layout. Benchwork construction does not require any tremendous carpentry skill, since only simple construction methods are used. If you take your time and work carefully, there should be no problems. What is important is that the benchwork be as solid and workmanlike as possible. The most spectacular scenery and finest rolling stock won't mean much if trains won't stay on the rails because of hurried or carelessly done benchwork. Which of the various benchwork types you use on the layout will depend on its size and the type of scenery and trackwork you have chosen.

TYPES OF FRAMEWORK

On small, simple, or portable layouts, a plain sheet of thick plywood can serve as both framework and sub-roadbed. For larger, permanent layouts, a more elaborate support framework is required. The two most commonly used framework types for larger layouts are butted-grid and L-girder.

Butted-grid framework is constructed of lengths of 1 × 2 (or larger) lumber running along the layout edges (girders) and crosspieces of similar size (joists), which run from side to side and across the ends of the framework (Fig. 6-3). If the layout is very wide, you may want to add another girder running down the center for extra strength.

L-girder framework takes its name from the shape of the girders used in its construction, which are shaped like inverted Ls. The primary difference between L-girder and butted-grid framework is that in L-girder the joists rest on top of the girders rather than being pinned between them

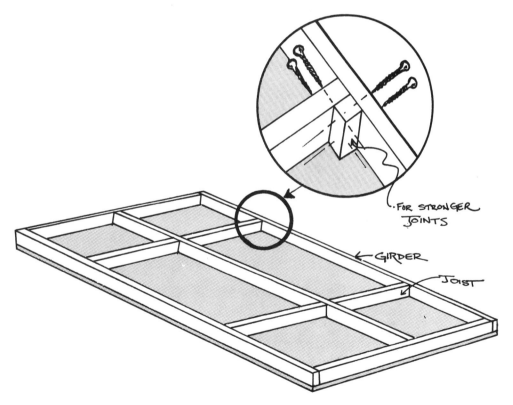

FOR STRONGER JOINTS

GIRDER

JOIST

Fig. 6-3 For small, simple layouts, butted-grid framework is an easy, efficient support.

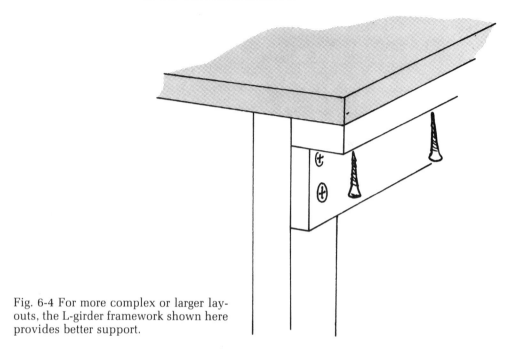

Fig. 6-4 For more complex or larger layouts, the L-girder framework shown here provides better support.

(see Fig. 6-4). Also, the screws that hold the joists in position are put in from below; as a result, it is a simple matter to modify, add, or remove joists at any time during construction without affecting anything on top of the layout.

Which framing method you use will depend largely on the details of the track plan. Butted-grid is excellent for smaller layouts and those using solid-top or cookie-cutter sub-roadbeds. It is easily put together, and, although it is less versatile than L-girder, it gives a good solid base for the roadbed. If you are building a larger railroad or one with a lot of mountainous scenery, a combination of L-girder framing and open-top sub-roadbed types will probably give you the best results. L-girder framing, although simple in design, will support a considerable area without requiring tons of lumber, and its versatility makes later improvements possible as the layout grows and your modeling skills improve.

A final consideration is the height of the benchwork. This is largely a matter of personal preference, but the layout will look more realistic when viewed from eye level rather than from above. A common application of this idea is to build the layout at a height where it can be conveniently worked on while standing, then operate it from a chair or stool that places you near eye level. Depending on your height, this usually results in a layout built from 36 to 48 inches above floor level.

TYPES OF SUB-ROADBED

The sub-roadbed supports the trackwork and provides anchor points for some of the scenery. Like benchwork, it must be built solidly and carefully to ensure proper train operation. The most common types of sub-roadbed used in model railroading are solid-top, cookie-cutter, and open-top. Like framework types, the type of sub-roadbed most suitable for your layout depends on the size, scenery, and trackwork of your plan.

Solid-top requires the least carpentry work because the entire layout is built on a solid sheet of plywood, often supported by boxed-grid framing (Fig. 6-5). The track plan can be drawn full-size on the plywood, and different track arrangements can be tried before you tack everything down. Solid-top sub-roadbed has certain disadvantages that limit its usefulness in layouts with elaborate scenery. It's difficult to raise track above the level of the plywood top and almost impossible to build track or scenery features below it. In addition, later modifications or repairs can be awkward, since all work must be done from above the layout.

Cookie-cutter sub-roadbed is similar to solid-top, but it allows track-work and scenery to be built easily above or below the base level of the plywood top. Like solid-top, a solid sheet of plywood is attached to the framework and the track plan drawn on it. Be sure that none of the screws fastening the top to the frame lies under the trackwork.

After you lay out the trackwork, make saw cuts through the plywood top along both sides of the track wherever it will run above or below the level of the top. Blocks of wood or risers can be inserted between the cutout track sections and the layout top to adjust the trackwork to the desired level. Once set, use screws and/or white glue to fasten the sub-roadbed firmly to the top and framework. Scenic features like rivers, lakes, or other depressions can be modeled by cutting out appropriate areas in the top to allow their construction below "ground level."

Open-top sub-roadbed consists of vertical wooden supports (risers) attached to the framework. These support the roadbed at the appropriate height. The framework between the tracks is left open later to be covered by scenery. Open-top sub-roadbed is especially suited for an L-girder framework, and it is almost universally used on larger layouts, where the cost of materials makes the cookie-cutter or solid-top methods impractical. Building a layout of this type requires some additional advance planning.

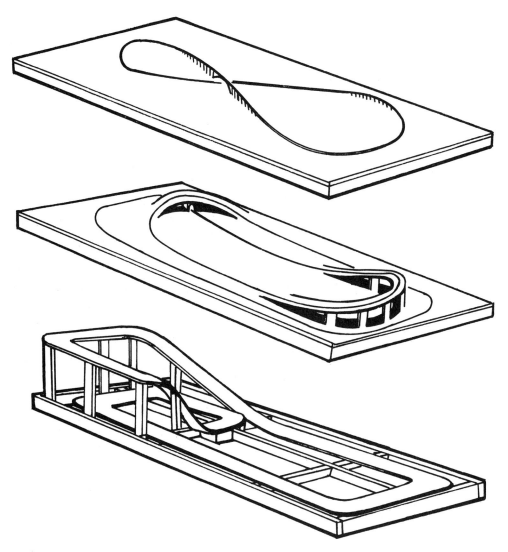

Fig. 6-5 Solid-top sub-roadbed is by far the simplest to work with, but it allows very little flexibility in the height of the track or in scenery features, such as lakes and excavations which are below ground level. A cookie-cutter sub-roadbed allows more natural variation in height, but is limited by the flexibility of the wood. Open-top sub-roadbed is the most difficult to use, but any arrangement of track and scenery can be duplicated. Note that the curves and slopes have been exaggerated in this drawing to show how the supports function.

You must determine the proper height for the risers at each support point and glue or screw them in place.

After the risers are in place, you must fasten and attach the actual sub-roadbed. There are several methods of making sub-roadbed. One, called ribbon style sub-roadbed, is similar to the cookie-cutter method. The track plan is drawn full-sized on a sheet of plywood, cut out, and then attached to risers. This is perhaps the simplest method, but it results in a great deal of wasted plywood. Lintel sub-roadbed uses strips of wood or plywood cut and spliced together to the proper shape and then attached to the risers. Spline-lattice sub-roadbed is made from two or three thin wood strips set on edge with small spacers between them (Fig. 6-6). Spline-lattice results in very solid sub-roadbed; however, it is difficult to shape around sharp curves and thus might not be suited to smaller narrow-gauge layouts, such as HOn30.

The type of benchwork most suitable for your layout will depend largely on its size and the type of scenery you have chosen to model. If you are building a small or relatively flat layout, such as an Eastern cranberry or plantation road, then butted-grid framing and solid or cookie-cutter sub-roadbed will probably be your best choice. If your pike will be hauling lumber or mine cars through the mountains and canyons of the West, then L-girder framing and open-top sub-roadbed would be best. The different types may even be combined to create different areas on the same layout, such as solid-top in level areas like yards or towns and open-top in areas of rolling woods or mountainous terrain. Whatever method you

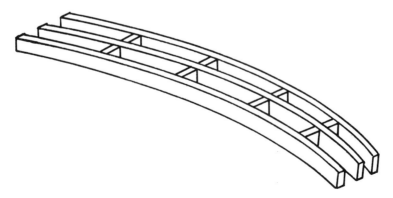

Fig. 6-6 Spline-lattice roadbed is very good support, but the difficulty of producing sharp curves makes it a poor choice for small-scale narrow-gauge railroads.

choose, remember to work carefully. Time spent now building solid bench-work will pay dividends in smooth train operations later.

TYPES OF ROADBED

Once you have completed the benchwork, the next construction step will be to lay down the trackwork. Although it is possible to fasten track directly to the sub-roadbed, using some type of roadbed material between the track and sub-roadbed will improve the appearance of your layout and help deaden train noise.

Numerous materials are used for roadbed. Two of the most common are Homasote wallboard and preformed flexible cork. Homasote is a pressed-fiber wallboard material sold at larger lumberyards. It takes track spikes, nails, or glue well, deadens train noise nicely, and can easily be cut and shaped to form a smooth surface on which to lay trackwork. It also will not warp when plaster scenery is added to it.

There are some disadvantages to using Homasote. Not all lumberyards stock it, although they may be able to order it for you. It comes in 4 × 8 foot sheets, which may be far more than you need, and like ribbon or lintel sub-roadbed it must be cut and shaped to fit your track plan. Always wear a dust mask when working with Homasote; although it cuts and sands easily, the dust can be irritating if inhaled. Also, if you are modeling main-line trackwork, the edges of the Homasote roadbed must be beveled to match the prototype roadbed. This is not always a concern in narrow-gauge, since many smaller roads did not ballast their trackwork as elaborately as the larger railroads.

Cork is perhaps the most versatile roadbed material available for use in model railroading. Preformed cork roadbed is made by a number of different manufacturers and is readily available at most hobby shops. It has the same virtues as Homasote and none of its disadvantages. It is flexible and easily fitted to your track plan, and it cuts easily with a hobby knife and is dust-free.

Cork roadbed comes in two strips that must be carefully split apart. Each strip has one beveled edge and one square edge. Laying two strips side by side with their square edges together gives you a length of single-track roadbed ready for use. Double-track (or wider) roadbeds can be made by laying down strips with their beveled edges together and then mating the square edges of other strips to the outer edges. Double-track roadbed can also be purchased ready-made from some manufacturers. Custom roadbed blocks for special trackwork (switches or crossings) can be purchased ready-made, or you can fabricate your own from sheet cork or extra roadbed strips.

Homasote roadbed can be fastened to the sub-roadbed with white glue and small ($\frac{1}{2}$ inch) wire nails, or with white glue alone. Cork roadbed requires both glue and nails to hold it in position until the glue dries. After you have glued the roadbed in position, set weights on it to hold it in place and allow the glue to dry overnight.

TRACKLAYING

Once the roadbed is in place, you can proceed to lay down the track. HO narrow-gauge track and track-laying supplies are available from a number of manufacturers. Track can be laid in one of two ways—by handlaying individual ties and rails and spiking them in place on the roadbed, or by using prefabricated track sections.

Hand-laid track is perhaps the most realistic in appearance, but it requires the most modeling skill to produce. Individual scale ties are attached to the roadbed and lengths of rail are then spiked to the ties, much like the way track is laid on prototype railroads. Great care must be taken to ensure that the track gauge (the distance between the rails) remains constant to avoid derailments, and hand-building switches and crossovers can be a time-consuming (although rewarding) task. Hand-laid track is not recommended for beginners; on your first layout, use prefabricated track and wait for a later project, when your modeling skills will be more developed, to attempt hand-laid track.

Prefabricated track is available in a wide selection of rail sizes and materials. I use nickle-silver rail both for its appearance and its resistance to corrosion; brass rail is less expensive, but it needs to be painted or darkened to hide its unrealistic color. It is also harder to keep free of corrosion. Prefab track comes in two forms, sectional and flexible.

Sectional track is often found in train sets and is readily available in a wide assortment of lengths and curve diameters. Because it clips together easily and requires no cutting, sectional track is excellent for a first layout. Several collections of track plans specifically designed for sectional track are on the market, and these often list exactly how many pieces of each type of track are needed for each plan. The only real disadvantage to sectional track is that it ties you to certain fixed-radius curves in your design. However, the almost unlimited number of possible track configurations should make it easy to find an interesting plan.

Flexible track is designed to be shaped easily to fit any track plan. It is particularly well suited to narrow-gauge layouts because it allows you to duplicate the often none-too-exact straightaways and curves of the prototype. The primary disadvantage of flexible track is that it sometimes must be cut into shorter sections to fit the plan or the rail ends trimmed evenly when shaped around a curve. There are a number of inexpensive track-cutting jigs on the market that greatly simplify the job; it would be a good idea to buy one of these if you plan on using flexible track on your pike.

Whichever type of track you use, the method of joining the rails together and to the roadbed is the same. Track sections can be clipped together with metal rail joiners, available at most hobby shops. Slip the joiner halfway onto the rail ends of one piece of track, then carefully slide the rail ends of the next track section into the joiners until the rail ends are butted together. Be careful not to crimp the joiner while slipping it onto the rail base. This will prevent proper alignment of the rail ends and can lead to derailments (Fig. 6-7). Be sure not to kink the joints between sections; too severe an angle at the connections can also cause running problems later. When using flexible track, you may have to trim away carefully the spikes holding the rail ends to the plastic ties so that the joiner can slip between the rail and ties.

There are several methods for attaching track to the roadbed. Most sectional track sections have small holes cast in the ties; small wire nails or brads can be driven through these holes and into the roadbed to hold

Fig. 6-7 If the joiners connecting the rails are crimped or bent, the rails can become misaligned, causing derailments.

the track in place. If you are using flexible track, you may have to drill holes in the ties yourself. A No. 60 drill works well for this, and a light hammer and a nail set are useful for nailing down track. Leave a tiny space between the tie and the head of the nail to allow the track to "float" in case the track expands or contracts as a result of temperature changes. It also helps keep the plastic ties from springing away from the rail and prevents vibration and train noise from being transmitted via the nail through the roadbed and into the underlying benchwork.

Track can also be glued directly to the roadbed with white glue or carpenter's glue. Run a line of glue onto the roadbed where the track ties will lie, clip the rail section in place, and then carefully position it in the glue. Pin the track firmly in place until the glue has completely dried. If possible, carefully set weights on the track to keep it firmly in contact with the roadbed as the glue dries. This method works well with Homasote roadbed and results in little or no train noise. Be extremely careful to keep the glue well away from all moving parts when gluing down switches.

When laying trackwork, keep all joints between sections as smooth as possible. It is a good idea to run a small file gently along the top and inside of the rails at each connection to smooth out any unevenness. As you work, frequently check the distance between the rails with an NMRA track gauge, particularly on tight curves made from flexible track. Leave a small gap between rails every two or three feet to allow for possible expansion or contraction of the roadbed. When using flexible track, avoid long stretches of straight roadway; a few gentle curves in a straight section are far closer to prototype and give the layout more visual appeal. Avoid sudden sharp kinks in your trackwork, since they will cause operating problems once trains start running.

Finish your trackwork with the same care you used on your bench-work. Even though you may be anxious to get the trains running, take your time and do the best job you can when laying track. The result will be smooth-running trains, which will make it time well spent.

BALLASTING THE TRACK

On the prototype, ballast serves to support the weight of the track on the roadbed and allows rainwater to drain away from the ties and rails. On a model layout, ballast helps bond the track to the roadbed, and it is the final visual detail that blends your trackwork into the rest of your pike.

Ballast can be applied either before or after the scenery is added to the layout. If it is done before the scenery is added, the track and ballast

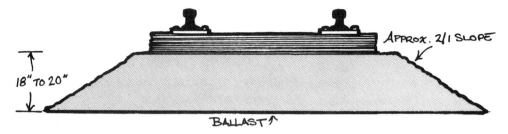

Fig. 6-8 In an actual railway, ballast serves the double function of giving the track a firm bed on which to rest and allowing rainwater to drain away from the tracks. The dimensions in this illustration are from an actual prototype line.

must be protected from later paint or plaster spills, but it is often easier to reach and apply ballast to some track areas before adding the scenery. You will have to decide which method is best for you.

Scale ballast is available from most hobby stores in a large variety of colors. Often main-line track ballast is gray, while yards and service areas are graded with dark gray or black cinders. Try mixing several close shades of ballast together to get a sun-bleached look, but avoid mixing light and dark shades together, since this will produce a salt-and-pepper look. Real ballast stones average two inches in diameter. Select ballast that will match your scale. One trick is to purchase ballast that is sized for the next scale smaller; for example, if you're modeling in O gauge, buy HO ballast. If you're working in HO, get N scale ballast. The smaller stones will improve the overall realism of the trackwork.

Ballast spreaders that slide along the rails automatically distributing and smoothing the ballast are available commercially. Ballast can also be spread by hand using a paper cup, a teaspoon, or a 3 × 5-inch index card. Sift the ballast into place between the rails, then brush it down to the level of the top of the ties with your finger or a stiff-bristled brush. Next, spread ballast along the outside of the rails and use the brush to sweep it even with the top of the ties and into a natural-looking slope away from the tracks. Check your reference books for pictures of ballasted track.

Work on about two or three feet of track at a time. Spread the ballast, bond it in place, and then start on the next section. Be careful to keep grains of ballast away from the moving parts of switches; ballast can jam the moving parts and can also act as a wick to draw the bonding glue into the switch mechanism.

The final step is to bond the ballast in place without disturbing your careful work. There are several methods of fastening down ballast. One simple method, and perhaps one to consider if this is your first layout, is to use dry ballast cement, available at most hobby shops. This comes in powder form and is combined with the ballast before it is spread onto the trackwork. Be careful to use the correct amount of cement and mix it thoroughly into the ballast. When the ballast is in place, gently spray water onto the trackwork. Once dry, you can glue the ballast securely to the roadbed and track. Another technique is the bonded ballast method. The spread ballast is gently but thoroughly sprayed with "wet" water (four drops of liquid detergent in a pint of warm water) and a bonding agent is then applied, which, when dry, holds the ballast in place without disturbing its appearance. One part white glue mixed with four parts water makes a good bonding agent. Mixing one part acrylic matte medium (available at most art supply stores) to three parts wet water also works well and has the added advantage of drying to a flat finish. Whichever you choose, use enough to wet the ballast thoroughly and ensure proper adhesion. The bonding agent can be sprayed on or applied with an eyedropper in confined areas; work on about a two- or three-foot length of track at a time. If the ballast dries out before you are able to apply the bonding agent, respray it and keep working. When you have completed one section, carefully wipe the railheads dry with a soft clean rag to avoid corrosion and ensure good electrical contact later.

Allow the bonding agent to dry overnight. If any loose spots appear after the ballast has dried, carefully rewet just that spot and apply some more bonding agent to the loosened area. As a final detail, grass or soil from the surrounding scenery can be worked up to the edge of the ballast to blend it into the scene. On spurs or little-used branch lines, weeds can be added to the ballasted area and even between the rails. Attention to such details will unify your trackwork and scenery and enhance the realism of your entire layout.

Off-the-Shelf
Narrow Gauge

KITBUILDING

Most model railroaders begin by building plastic kits, although a few have the nerve—and money—to dive into a wood or metal model. This chapter could be included with kitbashing, because every kit requires some detailing to make it more realistic. You can build a very credible model using a kit and the techniques outlined in this book.

Take the time to learn the basics of model building and become proficient at them before undertaking a more complex project. Building a kit properly requires considerable skill, and too often the modeler forgets the most basic rule: Read the instructions first! Trains are extremely complicated, and even the experts require guidance. You could build yourself into a corner if you are not careful. You may see ways to shortcut kit steps or to create subassemblies for painting, but always use the instructions for reference. After all, who is more knowledgeable about a kit than the manufacturer?

The assembly instruction sheet can be used to determine if you have all of the necessary parts and as a checklist during construction. Open the kit immediately after you buy it and check for missing or damaged parts. Nothing is more frustrating than to discover that a critical part is missing just as the project is coming to an end late at night or on a weekend.

If the kit is new, most dealers will replace it without any hassle. If you've had the kit for a while and it is partially assembled, you may be out of luck. Most manufacturers are pretty good about replacing missing

Fig. 7-1 After you have been modeling for a while, you will discover that you have begun to collect mountains of spare parts. Cabinets such as these are a good way to keep parts organized.

parts or even parts you may have damaged during construction. Send the part number, kit number, and some proof of purchase with a SASE large enough for the parts. It won't hurt to include a dollar or two for handling, plus a pleading note.

If the kit is rare, don't panic. It is relatively simple to fabricate or

Fig. 7-2 This tiny diesel is actually a Japanese prototype imported by Empire Pacific, but it looks exactly like the little Plymouths, Whitcombs, and Porters seen at industries all over America.

Fig. 7-3 This boxcar was built from scratch using scribed Evergreen sheet. Once a model like this is made, you could make a rubber mold and cast dozens of these in urethane to produce a string of cars.

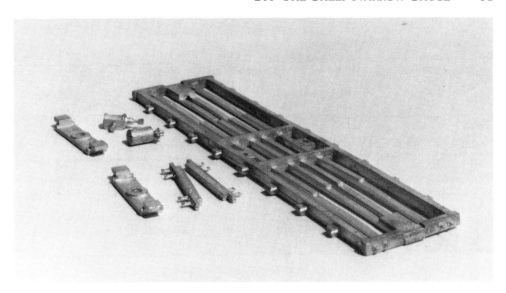

Fig. 7-4 Westco produces this simple flat-car kit in HOn3 and HOn30. In addition, you will need basswood in $\frac{3}{32}$-inch widths, trucks, and couplers, plus detail parts from Grandt.

repair most parts using techniques from this book. You may also find a similar part from another, less rare kit, or from the scrap bin you should be keeping.

CONSTRUCTION

Gather all of the tools you feel you might need and set them up in a clean, well-lighted work area away from the mainstream of other activities. Spread out all the parts and take inventory. Check all the parts and decide now if you want to modify or replace any of them with more detailed items. Many hobby shops have train-detail parts that you can buy individually. Set aside for now the parts to be replaced.

Cut the parts free from their plastic trees as you need them. This will help you identify them and keep smaller parts from getting lost. You may also find that it's easier and faster to clean off small parts and paint them while they are still attached to the tree. The tree is the best device for holding tiny duplicate pieces.

Filing

All parts should be test-fitted prior to assembly. Hold each pair of pieces up to a light and test for a uniform line of light. File or sand the

Fig. 7-5 Most payload models, such as this Chooch load of lumber, are made for standard gauge. This one has been cut off and narrowed to fit the flat car.

Fig. 7-6 Assembled Westco flat-car, ready for its load, which can even conceal weight or a sound-system speaker to ride behind the loco. To complete this model, add the lumber with tie-down straps or rope to secure it.

Fig. 7-7 A flat car can be the basis for an interesting tank car. Here a standard AHM tank with a platform has been added.

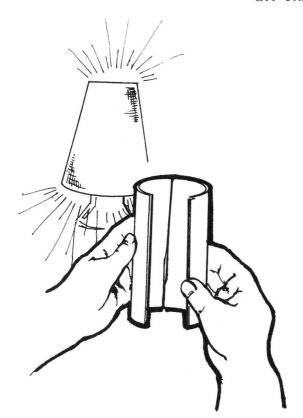

Fig. 7-8 Test-fitting the pieces to be sure they fit together tightly with no gaps.

parts until little or no light is visible, then fit the pieces together tightly. This procedure will ensure a good glue joint, and you will have less finishing work to do before the final painting.

A file removes material by scraping or abrading the surface. Lift the file on each backstroke and press lightly on the forward stroke. Never use heavy pressure or you'll clog the file teeth. Don't use pressure on the backstroke or you'll dull the filing edge.

Keep the file teeth clear at all times to get the smoothest surface with the least amount of effort. A file card (not the cardboard type) with wire bristles can be used to keep the file like new. Run the bristles into the file groove along their length until all foreign material is gone.

Before filing seam lines or putty, allow the area to dry completely. Otherwise, you'll clog the file and get a rough, uneven surface that will have to be sanded smooth later.

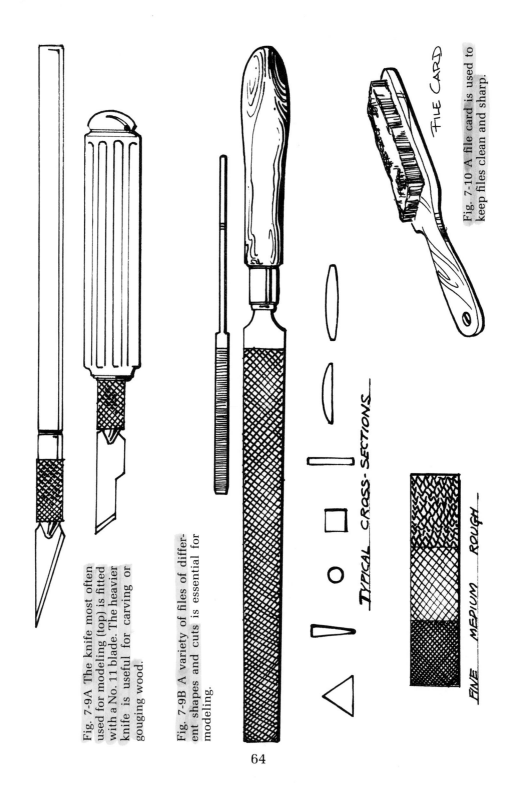

Fig. 7-9A The knife most often used for modeling (top) is fitted with a No. 11 blade. The heavier knife is useful for carving or gouging wood.

Fig. 7-9B A variety of files of different shapes and cuts is essential for modeling.

TYPICAL CROSS-SECTIONS

FINE   MEDIUM   ROUGH

FILE CARD

Fig. 7-10 A file card is used to keep files clean and sharp.

64

Scribing

Most train and building kits can benefit from scribing to simulate panel detail or planking. Manufacturers can save a considerable amount of money by simulating planking and paneling with raised rather than depressed lines. The reason for this is that the detail is cut into the female dies at the last minute, after the shape has been established. If they were to try and cut away everything but the fine raised lines required to produce a depressed line in the model, it would take many more hours of work.

Most new modelers scribe with the sharp side of the blade, but this will not produce a sharp line. The sharp tip tracks like a needle in a record groove and creates a V-shaped valley, with edges higher than the surrounding plastic. Usually, they have to sand the scribed area smooth and retrace their lines several times before obtaining good results.

The best technique for scribing is to break the tip off of the knife with a pair of pliers, as shown in Figure 7-13. Use the back side of the tip, keeping the knife nearly vertical, and drag it gently across the surface to be scribed using a straight-edge ruler for guidance. If you use the right amount of gentle pressure, you will have a continuous curl of plastic in

Fig. 7-11 The planking on the sides of this caboose was done by scribing styrene with an X-Acto knife.

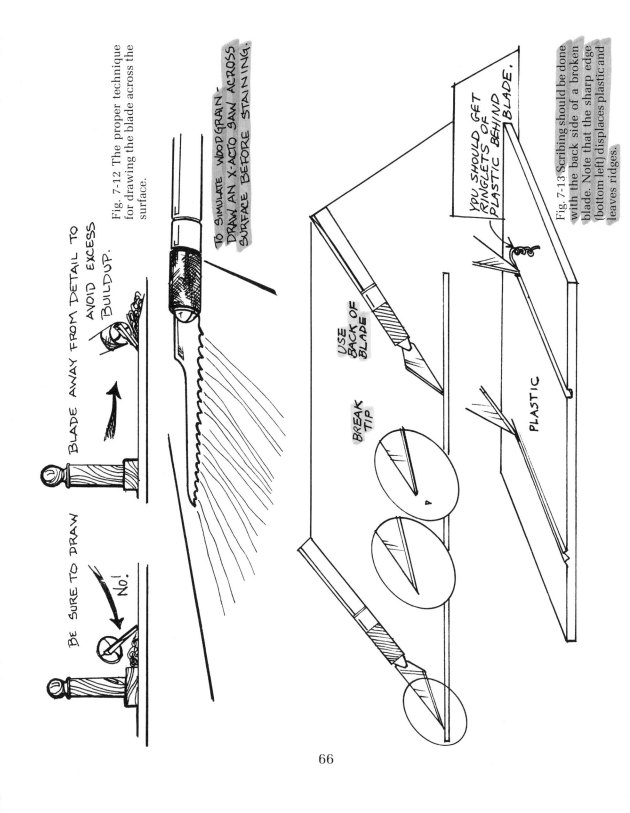

BE SURE TO DRAW

BLADE AWAY FROM DETAIL TO AVOID EXCESS BUILDUP.

No!

Fig. 7-12 The proper technique for drawing the blade across the surface.

TO SIMULATE WOODGRAIN - DRAW AN X-ACTO SAW ACROSS SURFACE BEFORE STAINING.

BREAK TIP

USE BACK OF BLADE

YOU SHOULD GET RINGLETS OF PLASTIC BEHIND BLADE.

PLASTIC

Fig. 7-13 Scribing should be done with the back side of a broken blade. Note that the sharp edge (bottom left) displaces plastic and leaves ridges.

front of the blade. The line will be rectangular in cross-section without any raising of the surrounding surface, so the finished model will look cleaner and crisper. Experiment on a scrap piece of plastic to get used to the procedure and to see how much better it will look.

Saw Cuts

Start cut lines by lightly dragging the saw blade backward over the edge of the part to create a slight nick. Press on the forward stroke to engage the cutting teeth and take firm, even strokes. After the initial cut, lift the blade slightly on the backstroke to keep from dulling the teeth.

Sheets of plastic can be cut up quickly by scoring. Scribe lines into the plastic by making many shallow cuts over the same line until you've cut one-third of the way through. Never use force to speed up the work; one slip with a knife as sharp as an X-Acto can cut you severely. Place the scribe line over a sharp table edge and apply pressure to snap the plastic along the line. Most types of plastic will break cleanly, but acrylic and Plexiglas may shatter. If the edge is too tough, clean it up with 320-grit sandpaper mounted on a smooth surface such as glass.

ASSEMBLY

Gluing

Hold two parts together and apply a drop of liquid cement or Hot Stuff at the top corner (assuming this is a plastic kit). Capillary action will draw the glue into the seam, making a good solid joint. Don't use too much

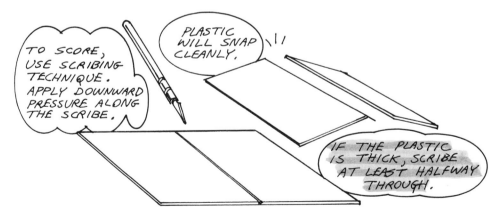

Fig. 7-14 One method of cutting plastics is to score the piece and then snap it along the scored line.

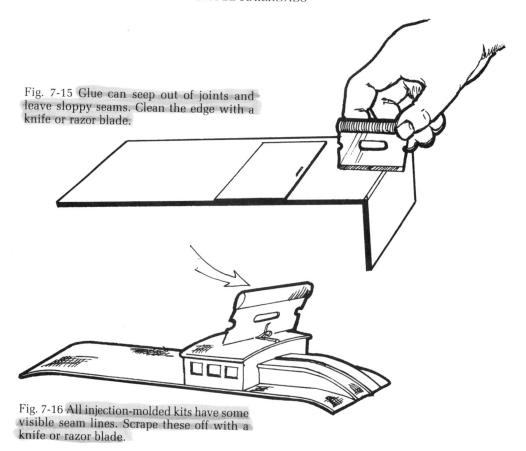

Fig. 7-15 Glue can seep out of joints and leave sloppy seams. Clean the edge with a knife or razor blade.

Fig. 7-16 All injection-molded kits have some visible seam lines. Scrape these off with a knife or razor blade.

glue or you'll weaken the joint and soften the plastic. Hold the parts together for a few seconds, or clamp them if necessary. Allow 24 hours for the glue to dry thoroughly; otherwise, the solvent will leech out and ruin your good paint job. The area that has been reworked will sink after the model has long been finished.

Using Plastic Putty

There is no easier way to fill minor seams, molding lines, or imperfections on a model than with the use of putty. Auto-body filler putty, Duratite Surfacing Putty, Green Stuff, and Duco Lacquer Spot-In Glaze are all excellent for putty work on models. Duratite Surfacing Putty is available in hobby shops and hardware stores. Green Stuff and Duco Spot-In Glaze are both obtainable from automotive parts houses and paint stores that handle automotive paint supplies.

A small artist's spatula can be used to apply putty to the model. Spatulas are available from art supply stores. The spatula method is best because it gives the smoothest application and reduces the chance of the formation of air bubbles.

When applying putty, be sure to apply it in thin layers and build up an excess, since it shrinks while drying. If you use putty for contouring, spread it far enough back on the body to allow the contour area to flow smoothly.

Putty should be allowed to dry for at least 8 hours for the best bond. Shape the area to its general contour with a file. When you have achieved the basic shape, sand the area with 400-grit wet-and-dry sandpaper to semismoothness. Remember to sand carefully because putty abrades faster than plastic. X-Acto's contoured sanding blocks are a great aid. When the area has been worked smooth by sanding, apply several coats of primer. This will show up any other imperfections. Reapply putty to fill these imperfections and set the model aside to dry for 8 hours.

Wet-sand the area again and apply several more coats of primer; then check the finish. You may find that still another application of putty is needed. Time and patience are the most important items in the building of a professional-looking model. When the area is free of imperfections,

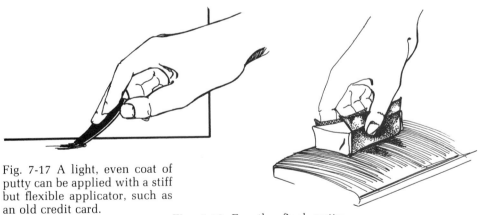

Fig. 7-17 A light, even coat of putty can be applied with a stiff but flexible applicator, such as an old credit card.

Fig. 7-18 For the final putty sanding, use a semisoft sanding block made from a spare chunk of RTV.

wet-sand to a final finish. Prime the entire model and prepare it for painting. Painting tips are described in Chapter 13.

Heat Molding

Every modeler soon comes up with a set of tricks to speed construction of a plastic model or to improve the finished product. Sooner or later, the one area that acts as a stumbling block to even the most experienced builder is that of extensive modification or reshaping.

Several products on the market are intended for use as a body putty, but they all have serious drawbacks. The first is to heat the plastic under a lamp or in an oven, which runs the risk of warping the surrounding plastic. Quick curing can cause the putty to shrink and crack as well. If too much putty is used, the area that has been reworked will eventually sink.

Another problem is the density of the putty. All of the putties on the market are porous and require special priming and sealing before a good finish coat can be applied. I have had models ruined because the reworked area appeared dull and flat compared to untouched areas. The obvious solution is to use a material as close to the original styrene consistency as possible. One solution has been to melt chips of styrene in acetone. But the problem here is that the solution takes a minimum of three days to cure, and the acetone crazes the surrounding plastic.

Using heat to mold the plastic appears to be the only quick and easy solution. Melting the plastic will make it pliable and easy to shape. Two pieces of styrene can be welded together into one piece that is many times stronger than a glue joint. The beauty of this method is that the joint or body work will be ready for a finish coat or sanding in 30 seconds. Obviously you must take care when using this method. Too much heat will melt all of the plastic beyond repair or at least warp it, causing a lot of unnecessary work. The fumes from melting plastic are toxic and can make you nauseated, but it beats the toxicity of glue.

SOLDERING

Soldering can be used for the assembly of brass parts or to hook up lighting and wiring. The proper technique is simple to learn and should be included in your repertoire of skills.

The equipment required for soldering is simple and relatively inexpensive. An expensive gun, such as the dual-range Weller, is not necessary to do a satisfactory job. In fact, some people find it to be too bulky for

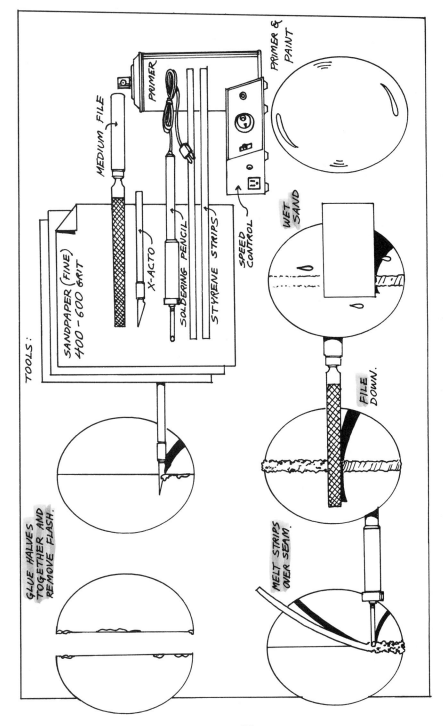

Fig. 7-19 Pieces of styrene can be joined with a soldering pencil for a quick, natural-looking joint.

modeling. X-Acto sells an inexpensive combination soldering pencil and hot knife that works very well. Some of the better soldering irons, the gun or pencil type, are made by Ungar, American Electric Heater Company, and Hexacon Electric. When choosing an iron, be sure that the tip will allow you to heat the work piece rapidly with a minimum of heat loss at the tip. For extensive work on large objects, a heavier tip is better, since the amount of heat stored at the tip is greater.

Both unplated and plated tips will produce good results if they are properly maintained. Unplated copper tips should be removed from the iron frequently and cleaned. To remove oxidation buildup, or scale, file the tip while cool. The file should be a flat, single-cut tooth type, such as the jeweler's Swedish file made by X-Acto.

Tin the tip before you use it by applying solder to the surface as soon as it reaches soldering temperature. Plated tips should be maintained by wiping the tip on a wet sponge and then retinning. Discard the tip when it can no longer be tinned. Clean either kind of tip by wiping it on a wet sponge after each soldering operation to prevent a buildup of flux.

Flux is a honeylike liquid used to help clean the metals being soldered and promote the flow of solder. Flux fumes are toxic and should not be inhaled. Be sure your work area is well ventilated. The flux used should be a noncorrosive type such as Sal-Met.

Lead-Tin Solder

The most commonly used solders are tin alloy, lead-tin alloy, lead alloy, and silver alloy. The most popular type is a lead-tin alloy of 60 percent tin and 40 percent lead. Ersin's Multicore solder contains five cores of noncorrosive flux, which makes it one of the most useful solders on the market. When aided by Sal-Met flux, it makes soldering a snap. Tix solder is good for small parts because it flows at low temperature.

Thoroughly clean the pieces to be joined with steel wool and denatured alcohol. Spread a minimal amount of flux on the surfaces to be joined. Apply heat at the intersection of the joint until the flux begins to bubble. Resin-core flux becomes active and removes oxides only when the metal has reached soldering temperature. Since the flow of solder is determined by its size, select a solder that will provide easy control: size 18 S.W.G. (.048 inch) works best for model assembly or wiring.

Feed small amounts of solder to the joint until you achieve a good fillet. Apply only enough solder to fill the joint. Too much solder will result in a weak joint. Avoid melting solder against the iron and flowing

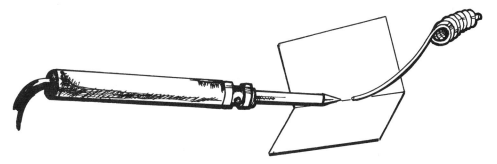

Fig. 7-20 Solder flows toward both heat and gravity.

it onto a surface that hasn't been sufficiently heated. When the right amount of solder has flowed, remove the solder wire, leaving the iron in place. Keep the iron on the joint for several hours to boil out any flux or impurities.

Remove the iron with a wiping motion, taking care not to disturb the joint. Allow the solder to cool completely before continuing. A good solder joint will be bright and smooth-surfaced, with solder feathering out to a thin edge. The joint will also be free of pinholes, craters, cracks, fractures, spikes, excessive solder bulges, and flux pockets. If the joint is disturbed while cooling, it will appear dull gray and rough-textured.

When soldering intricate parts, you must isolate the original soldered connections to keep from weakening them through the application of the additional heat. A heat sink is designed to radiate heat from unwanted areas and to keep the area cool enough to prevent solder from flowing into unwanted areas or from softening. Place heat sinks between any existing

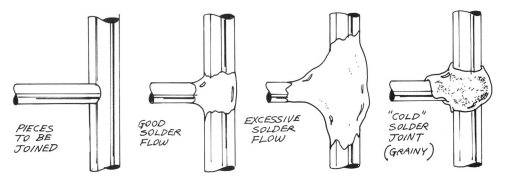

PIECES TO BE JOINED

GOOD SOLDER FLOW

EXCESSIVE SOLDER FLOW

"COLD" SOLDER JOINT (GRAINY)

Fig. 7-21 A good solder joint should be sturdy but not overloaded with solder.

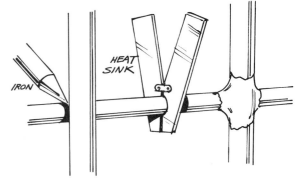

Fig. 7-22 A heat sink will radiate heat away from a previously soldered joint.

joints and the working area and solder in the normal manner. An alligator clip can be used as a heat sink in an emergency.

Flux residue should be cleaned from the parts within four hours after soldering, since it will become more difficult to remove the longer it remains. Remove all residue by brushing the parts with a medium-stiff brush, such as an old toothbrush, dipped in denatured alcohol.

Heat will oxidize brass and turn it a dullish-brown color. If you wish to restore the original luster of the brass, simply rub it with fine-grade steel wool and alcohol to remove the oxides. Then buff with rubbing compound and a soft rag.

Silver Solder

Silver solder forms the strongest bond short of brazing, and it is a better conductor of electricity than normal solder. Most soldering irons won't produce enough heat to melt silver solder. Instead, use a propane torch such as Westline or Bronson. They are inexpensive and long lasting.

A great deal of care should be exercised when using one of these torches. Read the instructions on the can and follow them religiously. Always use the torch in a well-ventilated area, store it in a cool place, and *never* puncture or incinerate the can.

To assemble the torch, close the valve and screw it finger-tight onto the fuel tank. Point the nozzle away from your body and any combustibles and turn the valve until you hear a faint hissing noise. Hold a lighted match to the end of the nozzle and adjust the valve until a small flame continues to burn. Allow the torch to burn on this low flame for at least a minute to warm up. Don't tip the can until after this initial warmup.

Afterward, the can may be tilted to any angle with safety. Regulate the valve until you get a flame two to three inches long.

Clean the pieces to be joined with denatured alcohol and steel wool. Apply silver-solder flux to both pieces and clamp them together. Hold the tip of the flame where the pieces intersect. Apply the silver-solder wire to the joint as soon as the flux begins to bubble and flow. Use only enough solder to form a small fillet. You can easily flow solder over a long distance by drawing the flame just ahead of the solder. Allow the soldered pieces to air-cool before handling. Use heat sinks to isolate joints other than the one you're working on.

Some types of low-temperature silver solder can be used like regular solder, but if you use them, you will sacrifice strength for convenience. Cerro Metal, sold in hobby shops, is easy to use for low-temperature soldering. Tix is a commercial product that is great for fine soldering quickly.

Wicking is the term used for removing excess solder from a joint. A braided or woven strand of wire is covered with flux and placed against the joint. Then heat is applied to the joint until the solder flows freely. Most of the solder will flow into the braided wire, leaving the area relatively clean. Clean the wicked area with denatured alcohol and a stiff brush. To remove all traces of solder, simply rub the area with fine steel wool.

Desoldering

Desoldering a joint for resoldering or removal is the simplest part of the soldering process. Heat-sink the area surrounding the joint. Apply heat to the joint and tug slightly on the wire or tube until it pulls free. If you wish to solder something else to the same area, use more flux.

Cross-Kitting

Scratchbuilding is the most rewarding type of modeling because you do it all from beginning to end. However, you can be creative with a fraction of the effort. Cross-kitting, or kitbashing, can produce unique models and is the closest you can get to scratchbuilding with commercial kits. This type of modeling gets fast results and produces a unique model, but it requires quite a bit of imagination, skill, and a little blind luck.

Kitbashing can be used for virtually any phase of modeling. You essentially work with shapes, and it doesn't matter if that shape is a plastic salt shaker or a carefully machined part, so long as it represents what you want.

To plan a conversion of any type, stick with kits of the same scale or at least ones that are close to one another. It's possible to get away with some variance in scale proportions part of the time. For example, the conversion of the Revell Tug (see *The Model Shipbuilding Handbook* also published by Chilton) uses parts from model trains ($\frac{1}{86}$ scale) and model tanks ($\frac{1}{72}$ scale), even though it started out as a $\frac{1}{96}$-scale model. The visual proportions are close enough when set up in the layout.

PLANNING EACH STEP IN A CONVERSION

Before starting the model, carefully plan out each step. Decide what you're going to use as a base kit and try to determine how best to approach the conversion. Gather your research material before you buy the first kit or part. Try to determine what parts are most important to the overall appearance of the finished model. These primary items will determine the

Fig. 8-1 This Train Miniatures caboose is a natural for conversion, with its wood sides, passenger-style windows, and cupola. The arched roof is easily narrowed and the seam is covered by a catwalk. By adding a baggage door in the blank area, you can make this into a typical Drover's caboose.

Fig. 8-2 The HO-scale locomotive (right) was converted from an N-scale engine like the one on the left. The enlarged cab was made from sheet styrene.

Fig. 8-3 The caboose has more charm and character than practically any other type of rolling stock. This one is nearly complete. I started with an AHM body shell stripped of all detail with an X-Acto knife. The body was narrowed by cutting out a section in the middle using a Zona saw. All of the equipment is just under an inch wide, although this will vary with gauge.

Fig. 8-4 The chassis was made of scribed sheet styrene and mounts HOn30 trucks by Grandt. The roof is covered with surgical tape to simulate canvas. The paint is Tamiya's new Hull Red acrylic, which flows on well even when applied by brush and is durable for handling.

silhouette and profile of the model. The other detail items are important too, but these are usually available or can be readily made from scratch. The idea here is that you want to create a jigsaw puzzle *without* all of the parts.

Buy the kits needed to build the completed model. Generally, you won't want to use more than two kits. As a professional, I buy enough kits to get the job done quickly. You will have to decide whether or not the expense offsets the ease of building the model. A collection of catalogs will probably help you make a decision on which models to scavenge.

Fig. 8-5 European trains are often four-wheelers, whereas U.S. trains are double-truck units. But most narrow-gauge lines had at least a few four-wheelers, and most N-scale equipment is European.

Fig. 8-6 Note the placement of the four-wheeled chassis for an American bobber. The chassis was simply filed flat on top and epoxied in place. The couplers are standard Kadee N scale.

Fig. 8-7 One would be hard pressed to recognize this as an E & B Valley D&RGW caboose kit now that it has been shortened and narrowed to become an HOn30 bobber for my Ridge Route Railway.

Fig. 8-8 This quaint bobber began as a cheap-looking Bachmann standard-gauge bobber. Add a European chassis, new paint, weathering, and extra detail and it becomes an asset to any roster.

Lay out all of the kit parts and decide which ones to use as is and which to modify. Isolate the parts that you will definitely use and place all of the other parts in a scrap box. You will be amazed how handy a scrap box will be for future projects. I've been collecting parts for so long that I have a huge parts cabinet with drawers designated as to type, shape, and scale of the part. I would be lost without these parts.

Try to use the kit instruction sheet as much as possible when building the primary shape. The less modification you have to do, the better. Basically, you will build the model in much the same way as a stock kit. As your skills improve, you will find this type of modeling enjoyable as an alternative to scratchbuilding.

Locomotives made for special gauges, such as HOn3 or HOn30, are usually well made, smooth-running, and unique. Unfortunately, it is just these attributes that make them expensive as well. It used to be that anyone interested in offbeat, branch-line, logging, or narrow-gauge trains had to buy expensive brass imports or model something less interesting. However, there is hope for the average modeler who doesn't have an unlimited

Fig. 8-9A This MDC caboose was easy to narrow because the body has internal scribe lines that can be followed with a knife. The sides were block-sanded smooth and square before being glued together. Note, too, how I cut and refit the cupola.

Fig. 8-9B The chassis was narrowed by filing off the sides until it fit snugly into the shell.

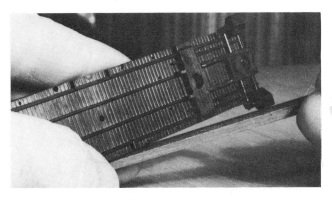

Fig. 8-10A I filled in the ladder holes next to the door with putty and replaced the stock part with a more detailed piece from Grandt. The trucks are Liliput parts investment-cast in brass with Con-Cor wheels. This gave me a long-wheel-base truck needed to match the appearance of the model in HOn30.

Fig. 8-10B This picture may appear identical to Figure 8-10A, but notice the subtle difference in stance between the HOn30 trucks and these HOn3 trucks from MDC. The 30-inch-gauge model has more overhang and typically sits lower to the ground.

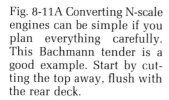

Fig. 8-11A Converting N-scale engines can be simple if you plan everything carefully. This Bachmann tender is a good example. Start by cutting the top away, flush with the rear deck.

Fig. 8-11B File the entire top section smooth. Fill the large cavity with a load of coal held in place with white glue. The wings are made of sheet styrene; the trucks are from an N-scale passenger car. Paint the entire tender with flat black, add decals and couplers, and you're done.

bankroll. Conversions of more common locomotives and running gear can yield models with all the finer points of brass models at a fraction of the cost.

The next three sections will show you how to take inexpensive models and produce some very special one-of-a-kind creations. In all cases, I tried to follow prototype practice as much as possible, if not actually modeling every nut and bolt of the original. My other criterion was to produce good-looking, reasonably priced models that would still run well. Surprisingly, I was able to produce better-running models using cheaper rather than more expensive kits. I've used Bachmann locomotives in many cases, and I want to stress that you should use the newer Bachmann models with metal side-valve gear rather than older ones. The early Bachmann models never ran well unless they were heavily modified. It's a credit to this company's engineers that it now has a line comparable to Minitrix, Kato, MDC, and Rivarossi (AHM).

A work of art—painted or unpainted—this brass and stainless steel Mason Bogie is from the Delton Locomotive Works of Michigan. The prototype was a double-truck locomotive for the Denver, South Park and Pacific Railroad, built and operated from 1877–1902 on both eastern and western narrow-gauge railways. The Breckenridge won the 1888 World's Fair award for the best machinery built in that decade.

The locomotive in the background is a standard gauge (O scale) Sante Fe diesel. The gray engine in the foreground is narrow gauge, demonstrating that you can fit an entire narrow-gauge train into the amount of space required for just the locomotive and a few cars in standard gauge.

One advantage of narrow-gauge modeling is the ease of displaying a train in
small scale. An attractive setup can be
built on an area as small as a one-foot
length of 2 × 4, as shown here.

The Durango & Silverton line hauled passengers and freight through the Rocky Mountains in its heyday. (Photo courtesy of Durango & Silverton Railroad)

This Western River Railroad model before painting and weathering certainly has that "plastic" look. Since the prototype train (see detail) is kept in pristine condition, I will paint the model and add only the slightest touch of weathering.

From this detail of a real Western River Railroad locomotive, you can see that not all narrow-gauge trains are dirty wrecks; this one is kept in mint condition, on public display in an amusement park.

The engine house was built from three Revell kits; clutter and debris add realism to the trainyard.

The converted train shed, discussed in Chapter 8; this picture shows how the roof and walls were weathered, painted and detailed.

This burned-out, abandoned building in the California desert is the type of subject not often included in a model layout. Such an addition creates a great deal of realism if you can duplicate the ash and smoke stains.

A Movie Miniatures brass kit, assembled, painted and weathered. Instructions for building the coal car are in Chapter 8.

Even though the subject is not especially colorful, the effects of a good weathering job are, nevertheless, evident in a color photo.

Trench trains can still be found in private use throughout the country and are often used as industrial shuttles.

The pillbox is part of a futuristic layout; the rich red colors found in the California desert add greatly to its realism. Note the stains in the rock from the drain pipes and the wreckage in the canyon.

Although now in service as a tourist ride and attraction, the Sugar Cane Train is typical of working narrow-gauge engines used to haul sugar cane on Hawaiian plantations. (Photo courtesy of Anything Photographic)

This rail truck was kitbashed for use on my Ridge Route Railway, using an N-scale Trix chassis. Like most narrow-gauge equipment, the prototype has received rough treatment.

This brass locomotive is so charming "as is" that it almost seems a shame to paint it. Many collectors specialize exclusively in unpainted brass engines.

Fig. 8-12A and B Either one of these N-scale locomotives can be made into a companion piece for the tender. I chose the Minitrix 0–6–0 (top) because the Bachmann 2–6–2 wasn't available when I started this project. Either unit works well.

LOCOMOTIVE CHASSIS AND ENGINE

Always start a conversion by making absolutely sure that the basic model runs well. Otherwise, you will never know if a poor-running model was a result of your handiwork or the factory's. You should also note that now is the best time to complain about a new model. Anything you do to

Fig. 8-13A Compare this engine to the ones in Figures 8-12A and B and you will see that the stock cab should be cut off just aft of the rear-most drive wheel. The cab can be made from styrene, sheet brass, or a conversion kit.

Fig. 8-13B If you use the Minitrix unit, use a Kadee front coupler and pilot-deck conversion kit. File off the original stack, domes, and headlight and replace them with brass detail parts in HO scale.

Fig. 8-13C Paint, weathering, and decals finish an excellent, easy conversion. This unit draws more attention at shows than anything other than my diesel, and yet it took only two evenings of simple work to complete.

Fig. 8-14 This interesting bit of motive power was a gift from Fred Hill, who got it in Japan. You could duplicate the design using a Bachmann chassis.

the basic model will void the warranty, even if your workmanship is not at fault.

Just for curiosity and comparison, try running the model straight from the box. The most critical test is to run it at low speed. Any piece of junk will function well at a scale 100 miles an hour, but it takes a good bit of engineering to produce a model that will creep backward through a series of S-shaped bends laced with Number 4 switches without stalling. I'd be willing to bet that it runs erratically and stalls and that the motor runs hot.

Run the locomotive at a moderate speed, one-quarter throttle, for an hour in each direction. If the motor gets too hot, break up the hour into ten-minute segments. After fifteen minutes or so, the model should speed up and run more quietly than it did at the beginning. This is a good sign and shows that it is breaking itself in properly. Do not lubricate anything until the initial time is up. You want the friction to lap in the parts for a smooth fit. Lubricating the parts only slows down the process.

After the initial break-in, completely dismantle the model down to the last nut and screw. Most models come with detailed instruction sheets to simplify this scary step. Place all of the parts in small bags or boxes to avoid losing them. Scrub all parts with denatured alcohol and an old toothbrush to remove metal shavings, grease, and dirt. If you have an ultrasonic cleaner (the vibrating type used for cleaning dentures and jewelry), the cleaning will be faster and more thorough. If you use a motor-

85

Fig. 8-15 How's this for some large iron on the narrow gauge? Believe it or not, there were many such units in existence at logging operations in California.

Fig. 8-16 The chassis conversion was frightening because the stock 2–8–8–4 from which this is derived costs $140. Fortunately, I got mine in sad shape for $15 at a swap meet. Actually, the conversion couldn't have been simpler. Cut the side-rod detail with nippers to isolate the rear pair of drivers on each truck. Remove the drivers and cut away the rear of the truck with a jeweler's saw. Butt the rear truck up nearly flush with the rear of the front truck. Measure the center-to-center mounting points of the trucks and cut out enough of the chassis to make up the difference. If you follow the photo and compare it to your model, the steps will be more obvious. Finally, shorten the drive shaft, glue the chassis halves together with epoxy, and reassemble.

Fig. 8-17A The body uses a cab, bunker, and domes from an MDC saddletanker. The saddletank is sheet styrene with strip styrene wrappers. Rivet detail is not important here, since many such boilers were welded. Add whatever details appeal to you in HO scale and paint the model.

Fig. 8-17B Add coal to the bunker (near) and Kadee couplers for realism. I will eventually add sound and lights and more detail to this unit.

Fig. 8-18A Here's an easy one. Jouef made a cute European four-wheel saddletanker, but it didn't run well, so I swapped the stock chassis for a Bachmann Docksider chassis. It looks better and sits slightly lower.

Fig. 8-18B Trim the chassis to look like this one until it will slip into the body shell. Note that the body had to be trimmed as well. Pack every empty space with weight and you'll have an excellent running unit. Tape-A-Weights from the auto store are cheap and heavy.

Fig. 8-19A Brass conversion kits are becoming popular now that brass prices are so high. This kit by Movie Miniatures is a typical Plymouth diesel, and it converts into one of the smallest running locomotives ever. The kit can be readily assembled with solder or ACC (Hot Stuff). Use a low-temperature solder such as Tix and a compatible flux. Clean and file all parts prior to assembly.

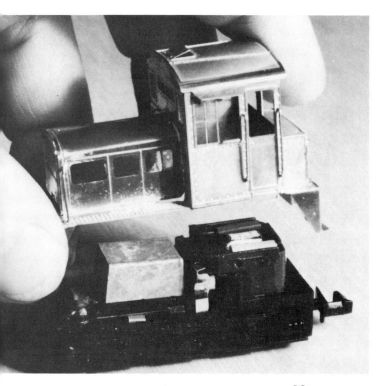

Fig. 8-19B The chassis will require very little for installation. Check the fit frequently to make sure there is no interference.

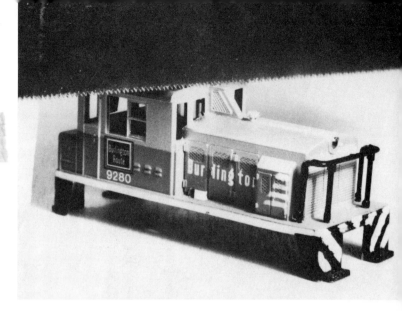

Fig. 8-20A Another variant can be made using the stock Bachmann MDT shell and the conversion cab. Cut the cab away just aft of the hood.

Fig. 8-20B Solder the cab and running boards together and glue them to the remaining parts of the plastic shell. Try to retain the original tool-kit area as well.

Fig. 8-20C Paint the body shell and detail using HO-scale parts. Note that even though HO scale is shown in most of these features, the same procedures work for any scale. In fact, O-scale builders profit even more because HO-scale chassis are cheap for conversion fodder; finished O-scale models cost a small fortune these days.

Fig. 8-21A Another loco that lends itself to easy conversion to HO narrow gauge is the Atlas/Rivarossi SW-1 switcher. I bought this one at a swap meet for $7 in perfect shape, while a new one would be about $35. Measure the HO cab and cut out the stock cab accordingly. Cut *less* from the area than you need to, and file to fit later. It's always easier to take away material than to add it if you made an error.

Fig. 8-21B In any conversion, one of the criteria should be to make the model run better as well as look better. Lubricate all parts sparingly with a quality lubricant such as LaBelle.

Fig. 8-22A Here's an FM diesel with a new cab, in this case a Movie Miniatures conversion kit. Bob Hayden has popularized similar conversions using old AHM HOn30 cabs from the Plymouth diesel. The style is similar to some of the lighter-weight GE units of 25 tons.

Fig. 8-22B Here is the finished Trix FM diesel. Most people can't believe the difference even when it's pointed out. The cab is a highly modified Grandt GE box-cab shell; the figure is a French soldier from an Airfix military model; the stack is made up of two pieces of brass tubing; and the couplers are a standard Kadee conversion kit. Oddly enough, the Kadee N-scale couplers are nearly perfect scale for 24- to 30-inch-gauge trains because they are slightly overscale, and narrow-gauge trains use smaller than standard-sized couplers.

Fig. 8-23A This decidedly European-looking four-wheeled gondola is made by Liliput for HOn30 use. I thought the lines were pleasing and bought it with an eye to an easy conversion.

Fig. 8-23B The interior of the gondola was detailed using Evergreen scribed sheet for the planking. The figure is metal from Walthers. I scraped off part of the German lettering and weathered the sides.

cleaning solvent, you can even clean the motor simply by soaking it in solvent.

Check all components for fit and ease of movement. You will probably never have another chance to do this unless the model quits running and needs a complete overhaul. With proper preventive maintenance, you

Fig. 8-23C The chassis is a spare Atlas freight car piece shortened to fit the shell. Kadee makes a separate chassis with couplers already attached. The trucks are brass Joe Works pieces from Empire Pacific.

Fig. 8-23D The completed gondola is right at home on any narrow-gauge pike in America. I still have to add a brake wheel. It only took one evening to complete.

Fig. 8-24 Here's one that's almost too easy to be considered a conversion. It is made in England and is considered N scale, but the body size is perfect and the trucks are even creditable for arch bars. It took fifteen minutes to convert the coupler, weather it, and remove the buffers on the end.

should never have to worry about the model. If there is any casting flash or sprue, remove it with a file or knife. Be sure to check all gear-mating surfaces and bearing surfaces, such as the axle journals.

Reassemble the model and lubricate all moving parts with an appropriate lubricant. Make sure you buy the lubricant at a hobby store and that it is compatible with plastics. LaBelle makes a good line of products designed specifically for trains. The gears should be lubed with a Teflon/silicone gear lube and rotated until all gear teeth have an even, fine film of grease. The key to proper lubrication is to remember that less is best. Too much will attract dirt, cause electrical difficulties, and ultimately could cause the gears to bind.

Motor and axle-bearing surfaces should get a single drop of oil each. To be safe, apply the drop to a pin, then to the bearing. Otherwise, capillary action will draw too much oil into the bearing. Be especially careful with oil around the motor, since any oil on the commutator brushes will ruin them. If you should accidentally get oil in the motor, clean it immediately with alcohol and test-run it alone with the gears disengaged. If it appears sluggish or erratic, clean it again.

Fig. 8-25 It seems to be standard practice to offer the narrow-gauge modeler dozens of Shays, Climaxes, and Porters to use in logging scenes, yet there are precious few logging cars like this one. I used a Russel log car detail kit, Evergreen styrene, Kadee couplers, Empire Pacific trucks, and some home-grown twigs.

Completely assemble the model to its stock configuration. This may seem like a waste of time, but it is the best approach. Test-run the locomotive again and give it the crawling acid test through those switches. Do you notice the improvement? You should see and hear a vast difference. With proper care, a ten-dollar Bachmann will run with the best Sagami-powered import.

If all is well, it's time to start on the conversion. Most of the examples given in the illustrations are simple enough for the newcomer and interesting enough for the expert.

PLYMOUTH SWITCHER

The Plymouth switcher is simple and has universal appeal. Gas-powered Plymouth, Davenport, and Baldwin switchers can be found everywhere in the world and yet they are not mass-produced. A few come close, such as the HOn30 model offered by ROCO, but this is a European type and not typically American. Joe Works also has the tiniest and cutest diesel around, but it too is more European or Japanese in flavor. Other manufacturers offer larger "small" switchers, such as Athearn's Hustler, but these are all made oversize to accommodate motors. Movie Miniatures offers a brass conversion kit that is very American, but it still requires an evening of assembly and modification.

Fig. 8-26A The MDC Sierra combine has been the basis for many of my favorite conversions. I like the short look as popularized on the Gorre & Daphetid and the real Sierra Railway. This necessitates cutting the body between the first two windows and an equal amount at the rear section for balance.

Fig. 8-26B The finished model of the Sierra combine. I chose not to make it into a Drover's style (with cupola), although I could have easily. Compare this to Figure 8-26A and you'll see how much a stock kit can be improved. The trucks are Kadee N-gauge four-wheel modern passenger trucks with talgo-mounted couplers.

Fig. 8-27 This is my favorite piece of rolling stock. The body is a radically shortened AHM standard HO combine with a narrowed and shortened MDC Sierra roof. The cupola is from an MDC Drover's caboose. The roof on this is tissue paper applied with white glue, but surgical tape, which simulates canvas, can be used instead. The trucks are Kadee N-gauge four-wheel passenger trucks with talgo couplers.

Before you start, decide what your options are. In HO scale, you will be using N-gauge chassis as a basis. In O scale, an HO chassis will provide the starting point. I will refer specifically to HO scale in these conversions, but the techniques are directly applicable to other scales. The best chassis to use in either scale is the Bachmann MDT switcher. Several other companies make virtually identical models, but none runs as well. Atlas makes the Davenport, which has a great grille and side rods, but it is probably the worst running of all types. The motor could be replaced with a Sagami, but that is expensive. What I did was use the detail parts and replace the chassis with a Bachmann unit. Surprisingly, the chassis are interchangeable.

Cut away the existing cab with a razor saw, being careful to follow all the existing lines. Make your cuts as clean and square as possible. Leave

Fig. 8-28 This SR & RL look-alike started as a monstrous E & B Valley model. The body has been narrowed and shortened. I even got two kits out of one by using some of the leftover parts to create a four-wheel bobber caboose! An alternative to Kadee trucks would be the beautiful brass ones sold through Fred Hill's Empire Pacific.

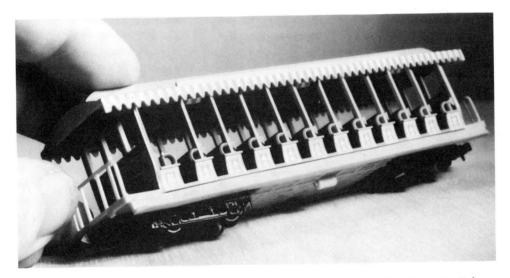

Fig. 8-29 From Japan's Tomy company, this is a model of the Disneyland train in Tokyo. The castings are a little heavy, but the model is typical of U.S. narrow gauge. You could also scratchbuild something similar using a flat-car or passenger-car chassis, just as the real lines do.

Fig. 8-30 Sometimes there are exciting discoveries in kitbashing. Although I was happy to get the rare Mantua diesel shell, I was concerned about a chassis to power it easily. To my surprise, the Athearn F–7 literally slipped into place.

Fig. 8-31 Although it is too unusual to use as is, the Liliput HOn30 0–6–2T can be modified into an American-style locomotive by changing the domes, stack, and cab. This unit runs well but is expensive compared to other makes.

Fig. 8-32 You may instantly recognize this old AHM HOn30 body shell. I replaced the 0–4–0 chassis that came with the model with a later-model AHM chassis. On future conversions, I'll use the Bachmann 0–6–0, 0–4–0, or 2–6–2 because they look and run better and are slightly cheaper.

Fig. 8-33 Over the years, a few companies have dabbled in conversion kits (myself included), but rarely have larger companies such as Peco. This kit is made entirely of white metal castings and converts the Arnold Rapido 0–6–0 into a European 0–4–0T HOn30 (00–9 in Europe) model.

Fig. 8-34 MRC-Nitto makes this great-looking Porter in O-scale, which will easily mount onto a Bachmann 2–6–2 chassis to create an inexpensive 2–6–0 Porter in On30.

the running boards, tool box, and side rails intact. Make a new cab from sheet styrene and Evergreen strips, or use a modified cab from another HO-scale model. This will give you a six-wheeled switcher with a low hood. It will not be exactly prototypical, but it is still interesting and authentic. You could improve on the look by removing the center pair of wheels and adding Grandt GE box-cab four-wheel side frames glued over the stock side frames. The hood could be raised by cutting it free of the running boards and splicing in strip styrene or pieces of another hood. These two additional steps will produce a credible model. Finally, add Kadee MT–1104 couplers in place of the toylike Rapido-style couplers.

The easy way out would be to buy a conversion kit. This would include all of the necessary body and major castings needed to create a nice replica of a Plymouth switcher.

Fig. 8-35A Not all narrow-gauge locomotives are powered by steam. The diesel has been used widely since the 1930s. The chassis here is an Atlas/Rivarossi unit that will remain unmodified except for Kadee couplers.

Fig. 8-35B The body has been shortened, lowered, and narrowed to fit the chassis and is only an inch wide. The finishing details will be similar to those on the MDC box-cab kit, although they will be finer and smaller.

Fig. 8-36 Most conversions require more ingenuity than skill. This model uses an MDC flat-car chassis, Kadee six-wheel passenger trucks, and an N-scale Pola crane cab with HO-scale details added. The trucks look like the heavy six-wheelers used on heavy equipment.

ROLLING-STOCK CONVERSIONS

Converting rolling stock to narrow gauge is not as involved as with locomotives because you don't have to make them operate. There are other problems, however. Some conversions can look awkward if they are not well thought out or properly executed. You can't expect to stick two-foot-gauge trucks under a standard-gauge streamliner body and call it a narrow-gauge model. On some conversions it is nearly that simple, but others are more difficult.

You should study the types of trains you want to model and decide what makes the particular style unique or interesting. Every line had a style as distinctive as a fingerprint. Once you become experienced, you will be able to tell in an instant if a model was patterned after The Naciónales de Mexico, the Maine Central, or the Denver & Rio Grande.

The most important part of the look is the ratio of height, length, and width. For example, the Maine trains were two-foot gauge and the cars were usually 6 feet 6 inches wide by 7 feet tall by 26 to 28 feet long. Since

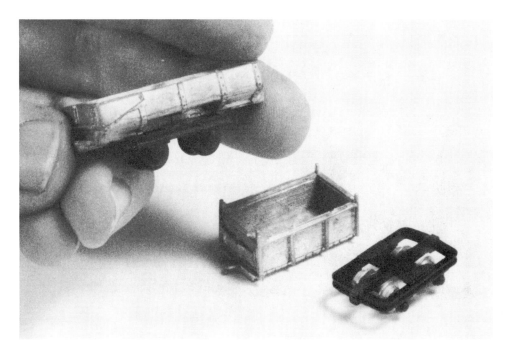

Fig. 8-37 My railroad has a combination of precious ore, coal, and lumber as revenue sources. Therefore, I need a lot of diminutive rolling stock. These white metal ore-car kits are mounted on AHM HOn30 chassis that have been narrowed to run on Z-gauge track, thus producing HOn18! Eighteen-inch trains are often used in mines, where space is at a premium. The chassis are easy to regauge by sliding the wheels on the axles.

Fig. 8-38 These HOn30 ore cars are basically weathered N-scale items with HO scale ore loads and Kadee couplers.

Fig. 8-39 Some N-scale cars are almost useful as is without any modifications, except to add HO-scale brake wheels and Kadee couplers. Note that the FMC car has both styles of couplers mounted. It is used in a mixed consist to mate my cars with someone else's. The CN car next to the HO-scale locomotive looks perfectly natural.

we can get only 2-foot 6-inch gauge trucks, we have to make a concession and increase the height and width of the car by 6 inches to retain the ratio.

After you've been building models of this type for a while, you will have backlogged information, parts, and the intuition needed to build most of your rolling stock from imagination. Meanwhile, you will have to study books and catalogs to find the right combination of parts needed to achieve a certain look. But that's also part of the fun. An example would be a four-wheel bobber. Fortunately, there are many N-gauge four-wheel chassis available. Simply scout around until you find one with the correct look and length. Longer, heavier cars, such as the ore cars, have the best chassis since they are proportionately larger than an N-scale bobber caboose chassis. With this in mind, let's look at a four-wheeled caboose as one of the easier conversions.

Fig. 8-40A and B These excellently detailed engines are only one and a half inches long! They are excellent examples of the amazing amount of detail possible in N-scale. Photographs by Thoen Photography.

Bobber Caboose

The bobber caboose has been a virtual standard for bringing up the rear on narrow-gauge trains. It is generally small, easy to build and always four-wheeled. I have built a caboose on a single freight truck (see Fig. 8-8) and Kadee has its design in HO scale.

There are literally dozens of different styles of bobbers. The sky is the limit: after all, you are the shop foreman and can do what the real foremen did—use whatever is handy. The most common style is the simple box of wood with small ventilation and viewing windows at each end. The most exotic would be like the one I built, using an N-gauge European chassis with end platforms, identification markers, cupola, chimney pot, roof walks, and so on. What I did was to condense the styling of a standard-gauge eight-wheeler in the tradition of Walt Disney's trains. The emphasis is on character.

Research the model and sketch it out prior to construction. I first made a crude cardboard mockup to check proportions, because it's very easy to make a mistake and produce a clumsy shape. There is a thin line between the two and it's very subjective: what is cute to you may be ugly to someone else. I really enjoy most of the conversions I've done and they never fail to draw comment from visitors. Be creative, and you should have one of the more enjoyable model-building projects possible.

Scratchbuilding

Many of the procedures and techniques outlined in this chapter are used by professionals for scratchbuilding. Whenever you modify a kit to any great extent, you are scratchbuilding. But at what point one becomes the other is difficult to determine. You should not attempt to scratch-build models until you are thoroughly familiar with basic modeling techniques.

Technically, a scratchbuilt model is one that doesn't use any commercially available parts in its construction. However, anyone would be foolish to machine an entire locomotive out of solid brass when there is a great variety of commercial parts available.

WOODCARVING

Woodcarving is sometimes necessary as a step toward achieving another end. I'll frequently carve a shape out of a hardwood such as bass or jelutong and use it as a master or buck to produce a vacuum-formed piece, a Fiberglas shell, or as a base to add sheathing.

A good set of woodworking tools from a craft shop is essential for doing a good job. You will need several sizes and shapes of chisels, a plane, a hobby knife, files, a Surform, and possibly a Dremel moto-tool.

To make the buck, screw two planks of wood together to form a block. This is easier than using one large piece, and it will give you an accurate center line to work out from. Then you can separate the halves later to form left- and right-side molds. This method is far easier than trying to cut a block down the middle after you have done the painstaking preliminary work.

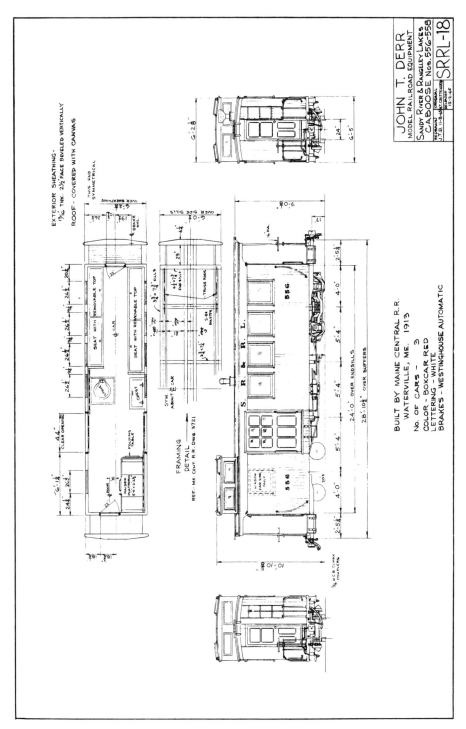

Fig. 9-1A, B, and C Using plans such as these (shown here reduced in size over three pages), a dedicated modeler can build unique locomotives and rolling stock that are available in no other form.

109

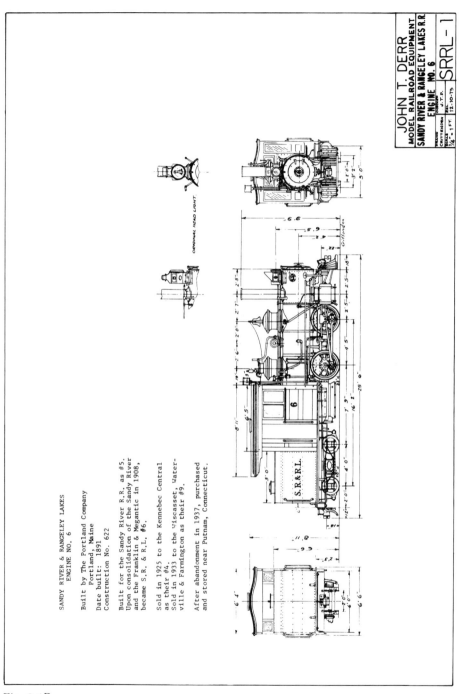

SANDY RIVER & RANGELEY LAKES
ENGINE NO. 6

Built by The Portland Company
Portland, Maine
Date built: 1891
Construction No. 622

Built for the Sandy River R.R. as #5.
Upon consolidation of the Sandy River
and the Franklin & Megantic in 1908,
became S.R. & R.L. #6.

Sold in 1925 to the Kennebec Central
as their #4.
Sold in 1933 to the Wiscasset, Water-
ville & Farmington as their #9.

After abandonment in 1937, purchased
and stored near Putnam, Connecticut.

JOHN T. DERR
MODEL RAILROAD EQUIPMENT
SANDY RIVER & RANGELEY LAKES R.R.
ENGINE NO. 6
SRRL-1

Fig. 9-1B

110

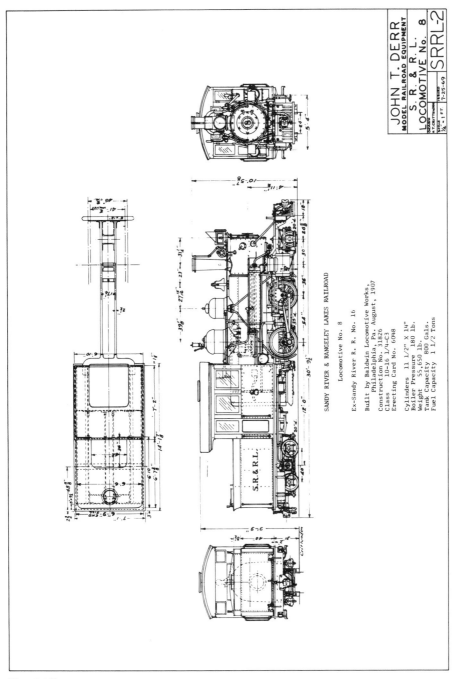

SANDY RIVER & RANGELEY LAKES RAILROAD

Locomotive No. 8

Ex-Sandy River R. R. No. 16

Built by Baldwin Locomotive Works,
Philadelphia, Pa. August, 1907
Construction No. 31826
Class 10-16 1/4-C3
Erecting Card No. 6048

Cylinders 11 1/2" X 14"
Boiler Pressure 180 lb.
Weight 55,650 lb.
Tank Capacity 800 Gals.
Fuel Capacity 1 1/2 Tons

JOHN T. DERR
MODEL RAILROAD EQUIPMENT
S. R. & R. L.
LOCOMOTIVE No. 8
SRRL-2
DRAWN
H.T. CRITTENDEN
SCALE
1/4" · 1 FT
7-25-69

Fig. 9-1C

111

Fig. 9-2 This model of a launch gantry at the Kennedy Space Center at Cape Canaveral was completely scratchbuilt using Plastruct structural shapes.

Sand the buck smooth with dry 400-grit sandpaper and coat it with Dope sanding sealer and Dope filler. Apply two or three coats and allow each coat to dry between applying another. Sand the final surface with wet 600-grit sandpaper. You'll be amazed at how smooth the wood can be. This sealer will also take glue, so you can add plastic detail items prior to making a mold.

Other than mold making, you will do very little woodcarving. Many items that are made of wood on the prototype will often look better on the model if they are made from some other material, such as styrene plastic. The reason is that most woods suitable for detailed model use have large, obvious grain patterns. The exceptions are bass and thin hardwood veneers.

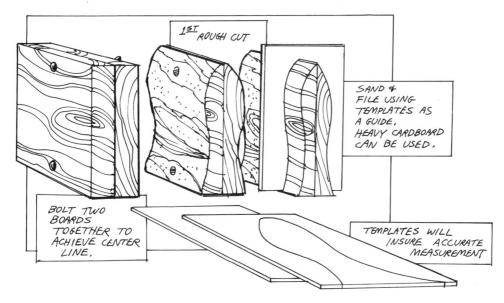

Fig. 9-3 Using a template to form a model from wood.

MAKING RUBBER MOLDS

Making rubber molds for relatively small parts is easy. The best type of mold material to use is Silastic "A" by Dow Chemical Company.

Whether or not you are using a kit or a scratchbuilt master, you must first block off all holes that go through the piece. Paper rubber-cemented to the back of the piece works well to prevent the two halves from joining. Do not use an oil-base clay, since it will retard setup time on the rubber.

The next step is to divide the piece in half, as shown in Figure 9-4. Build up a box around it using illustration board or poster board, which can be acquired at any stationery or art supply store. White glue such as Wilhold or Elmer's works perfectly with the board. The top of the box should be at least $\frac{1}{2}$ inch higher than the top of the piece to be molded.

To determine how much mold material to use, fill the box with table salt to about $\frac{1}{4}$ inch over the top of the buck. Pour the salt into a paper cup and mark the amount with a pencil. Be sure to empty out all excess salt from the mold and cup.

Mix the Silastic according to the manufacturer's directions and slowly pour it into the box. Gently shake or tap the box to release any air bubbles.

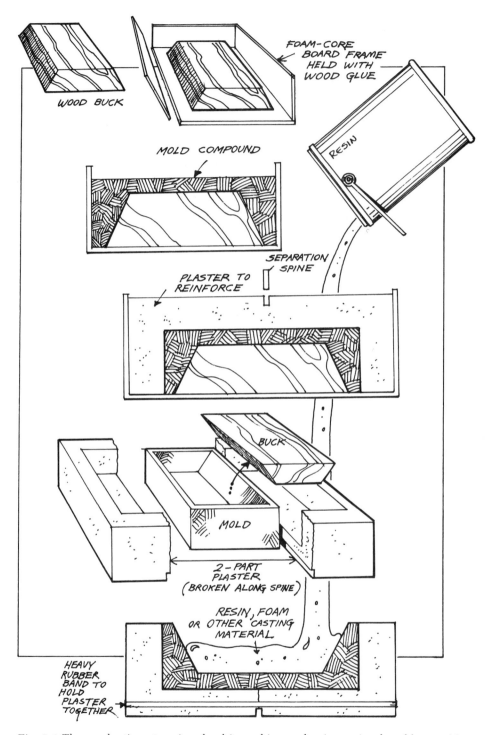

WOOD BUCK

FOAM-CORE BOARD FRAME HELD WITH WOOD GLUE

RESIN

MOLD COMPOUND

SEPARATION SPINE

PLASTER TO REINFORCE

BUCK

MOLD

2-PART PLASTER (BROKEN ALONG SPINE)

RESIN, FOAM OR OTHER CASTING MATERIAL

HEAVY RUBBER BAND TO HOLD PLASTER TOGETHER

Fig. 9-4 The production steps involved in making and using a simple rubber mold.

Let the Silastic set for about 24 hours, or as recommended by the manufacturer.

When the first half has set up completely, remove all the illustration board. Don't worry about trying to save the board; it's not worth it.

Build a new box around the first half, approximately 1 inch wider. Do not use the salt this time; it should require the same amount as the first measurement.

Before pouring the second layer of Silastic, use mold release only on the exposed mold material. I use a colored lacquer spray paint so that I can see that I have completely covered the mold. Do not spray the paint on the part. Paper or Saran Wrap, carefully cut, can act as a separating agent instead of a liquid mold release.

Let the second half of the mold set up properly before removing the illustration board and separating the two halves.

Cut a pour hole into the rubber about $\frac{1}{4}$ inch in diameter. Hold the halves of the mold together with rubber bands.

For actual casting, use casting resin that has been warmed to about 80 degrees F. For complicated parts, it is sometimes best to paint the resin into the mold halves before putting them together and pouring in the remainder. For best results, let the resin set up overnight before opening the mold.

LOST WAX CASTING

The first step in lost-wax casting is to prepare a wax master, or pattern, of the mold. Using wax and a warm artist's spatula, shape the part exactly the way you want it to look. Pins and small pieces of wire and scrap can be used to shape the pattern. Use dental wax, which comes in sheets about $\frac{1}{4}$ inch thick and can be purchased at dental supply houses.

Work as much detail as you want into the pattern, since this process allows you to get the finest details. If you plan to use the finished mold more than once, make sure to angle (draft) the parts so that they will pull out of the mold easily. If the part is complex or has undercuts, you may have to break up the mold to get the part out.

Place the finished pattern on the sheet and form a box around it to form one-half of the mold. Place the part face down and pour in mixed plaster of paris. Before mixing the plaster, sift it to get rid of lumps. When

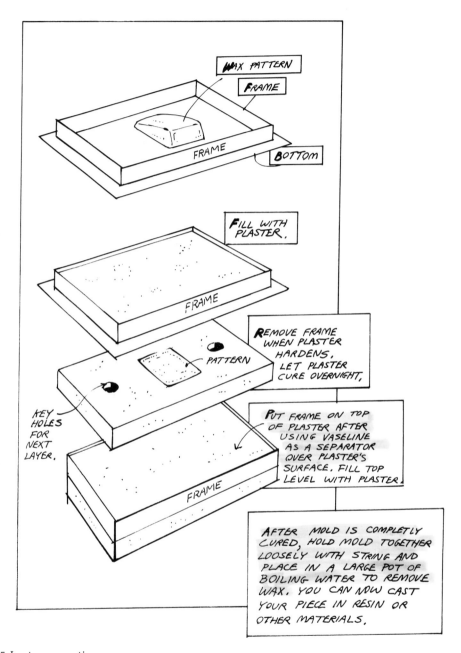

WAX PATTERN

FRAME

FRAME

BOTTOM

FILL WITH
PLASTER.

FRAME

PATTERN

REMOVE FRAME
WHEN PLASTER
HARDENS.
LET PLASTER
CURE OVERNIGHT.

KEY
HOLES
FOR
NEXT
LAYER.

PUT FRAME ON TOP
OF PLASTER AFTER
USING VASELINE
AS A SEPARATOR
OVER PLASTER'S
SURFACE. FILL TOP
LEVEL WITH PLASTER.

FRAME

AFTER MOLD IS COMPLETLY
CURED, HOLD MOLD TOGETHER
LOOSELY WITH STRING AND
PLACE IN A LARGE POT OF
BOILING WATER TO REMOVE
WAX. YOU CAN NOW CAST
YOUR PIECE IN RESIN OR
OTHER MATERIALS.

Fig. 9-5 Lost-wax casting.

buying plaster of paris, also get a package of plaster hardener to make a stronger mold.

Allow the mold half to cure and dry at least overnight. It can then be removed from the box and the base taken off. The wax pattern is embedded in the plaster and turned right side up.

Gouge two holes on either sides of the wax pattern, as shown in Figure 9-5. These holes will be filled with plaster when the second half is poured and will enable you to line up the mold halves.

Place the mold frame on top of this first half to make the second. Dust the mold surface with dry plaster so that the halves will separate easily when dry. Pour a mixture of plaster into the frame and again allow it to cure.

At this point, you have the finished mold with the wax pattern inside. Tie the halves loosely with string and put the whole works into a pot of boiling water. The wax then becomes "lost" as it melts out of the mold cavity. All of the sharp, fine details are left in the clean cavity.

To make the part, mix powdered dental plastic with thinner. (Both can be obtained at dental supply houses, along with tips on their use.) Make a thick putty and poke this into the cavity. Be sure to make enough to fill the cavity. Next, close the mold and press it together. Heat the mold in a 150-degree oven to cure the plastic. Allow the part to cool and carefully remove it from the mold. Use the part as you would any normal plastic piece.

RESIN CASTING

Casting resin is a transparent, liquid plastic that upon curing is glass-like and clear. Casting resin can be a useful material for the hobbyist as well as for the professional. To be successful with it, you must work slowly and carefully and keep the molds and equipment clean. With experience, you'll gain speed. Practice first with simple molds, then try more detailed forms. Use flexible molds that will bend or stretch to release the casting, or use one- or two-piece plaster and metal molds.

The surface of the mold will be reproduced in reverse in the casting. For example, an indented scratch in the mold will produce a raised line in the casting and vice versa. A dull-surfaced mold will produce a dull-surfaced casting; a highly polished mold will produce a highly polished casting.

As soon as you are finished, clean all tools and brushes with cleaner or acetone to prevent the resin from hardening on them.

METAL DIE-CASTING

Most hobbyists prefer the look, heft, and durability of metal parts over plastic. You can create your own metal parts after first making a master from any of the materials discussed above. The next step is to create an RTV rubber mold (see Figure 9-6). (RTV stands for Room Temperature Vulcanizing, or "cold-cure" rubber.) You'll need a two-part mold to form one solid three-dimensional piece. Support the object to be molded on straight pins to elevate it above the box base or surround it with water-based clay (low-temperature firing clay). Fill the box until it covers the object halfway and let it cure for 6 to 8 hours.

Spray the object and mold with mold release. This will form the break line for the mold. Pour in the remainder of the RTV, covering the object; let it cure for 6 to 8 hours.

Strip away the box and separate the two halves. Look for any imperfections. Cut vents to allow air and gas to escape from the mold, and cut a V-shaped trench for a pour hole. If any metal should seep out of these holes, it can be filed off later.

The large cutout will be the pour hole for the molten metal. This should be quite large and positioned in an area where it easily can be filed away later. The metal I use is nothing more than 60-40 coreless (tin and lead) solder, which you can find as bar stock in any hardware store. A few dollars' worth will be enough for several figures.

You'll need a disposable pan to heat the solder to the melting point over an open flame. **Caution:** Do not use the pan for food after using lead solder. *Be extremely careful of the molten metal:* it can cause severe burns. It may take a few minutes for the metal to melt, so put it on the stove before proceeding with the next step. Don't worry about using too much; the excess can be remelted later for another project.

Wrap the rubber mold with rubber bands to hold it together. Use a vise as well if the object is large, since the mold could expand and distort the object.

Stand the mold upright and slowly pour in the molten metal. Be careful that you don't burn yourself. If the object being formed is large or the rubber is thick, heat the mold in an oven set at 200 degrees prior to filling it with metal.

Wait several minutes for the object to cool slightly. If you are too eager, there could still be molten metal in the mold or the object will warp. If you want more than one object, pour it now while the mold is still hot. This will save you trouble later and the image will be sharper. Do not

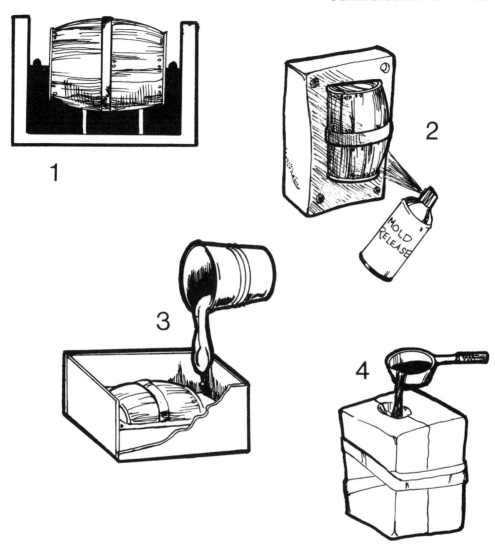

Fig. 9-6 Metal die-casting. (1) Water-base clay supports the object; mold is then filled with RTV. (2) Spraying with mold release creates the break line. (3) Remaining RTV compound is added and allowed to cure. (4) A funnel-shaped hole in the top of the mold is used to pour in the molten metal.

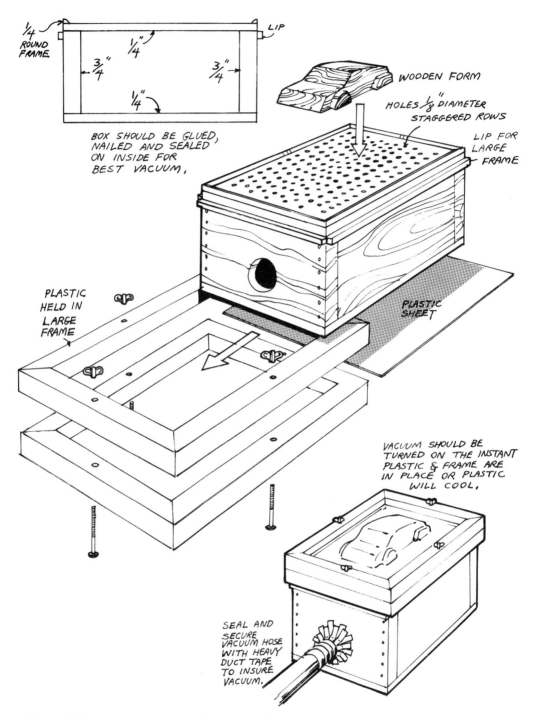

Fig. 9-7 The equipment needed for vacuum forming is easily constructed.

120

inhale fumes from the rubber, since they are toxic. Finish the object as you would any commercially cast item.

VACUUM FORMING PLASTIC

The average model railroader can use vacuum forming for many things. Vacuum forming plastic may sound like a complicated technique, but it's actually simple if you have the right equipment. Figure 9-7 shows how to construct the necessary equipment.

The setup for the technique is the same as that used with a Mattel Vacuum Former. The only difference is that here you can use various thicknesses of plastic in larger sizes, and a vacuum cleaner supplies the drawing power instead of a hand pump.

After the box is made, make a master for the object you want to duplicate in plastic. The object must be no more than a few inches tall, and it can't have any undercuts (areas that are less than vertical). As many surfaces as possible should have an angle of 5° off vertical so that you can pull off the mold without damaging the piece. Make a base ¼-inch high to fit around the molded part to give you some excess for a cut line later.

You can heat the plastic with a light bulb, heat gun, hair dryer, or area heater. The best would be heated coils, such as those found in an electric oven. Just be careful that the plastic doesn't start to smoke or catch fire. Styrene produces poisonous fumes when it burns. Heat the plastic and watch it constantly. Plastic will first wrinkle and curl up, then it will start to drape. It's during the drape cycle that you want to place it quickly over the form and start the vacuum. If the part doesn't come out with crisp detail, check the amount of draw.

Bridges and Trestles

Bridges add excitement to a model railroad, providing a reason for changes in track elevation and giving an opportunity for such interesting terrain as small streams and creeks or rugged mountain cliffs. However, bridges on a model railroad differ greatly from those on a real one. The real railroads built bridges only when absolutely necessary, whereas model railroads often try to include as many bridges as possible in their layout designs.

If you are modeling a narrow-gauge line, you can probably get away with having more than one bridge on a layout. Most narrow-gauge railways had bridges of all types because of the terrain they traveled, but don't get carried away. Too many bridges on one layout can look unrealistic.

The best way to create a truly credible scene is to study the prototype of the railroad you are modeling and see how bridges are used on their lines. Don't purchase a bridge just because you like the way it looks. You may have trouble later fitting it into the scenery and coordinating it to suit the railroad prototype. Bridges are a custom addition to a layout and should be chosen carefully.

If you decide to model a long-span bridge for your layout, such as a cantilever or continuous, or if space on the layout is extremely limited, you might want to use the technique of selective compression to reduce its dimensions. Most of the bridges found on actual railroads are too long and the valleys too deep for most layouts. To compress selectively a prototypical bridge, use its true-to-scale width, height, and timber dimensions, and simply reduce the length of the bridge to a more suitable size.

A few factors should be taken into consideration when choosing the

Fig. 10-1 Believe it or not, this 1869 scene of Devil's Gate Bridge can be re-created using the techniques outlined in this chapter. Courtesy of Union Pacific Railroad Museum Collection; photo by A. J. Russell.

correct bridge for your layout: the time period being re-created, the load and traffic requirements, and the location and terrain.

The time factor is perhaps the easiest to solve because by this point you should have already decided upon a specific era in which the scene takes place. The period of time you choose will closely govern your choice

123

Fig. 10-2 Engine No. 119, with a full head of steam, works its way up to meet the Central Pacific over a newly completed trestle. Courtesy of Union Pacific Railroad Museum Collection; photo by A. J. Russell, 1869.

of bridges; you need only decide upon the material and design in relation to what was available at that time.

For load and traffic requirements, you will have to decide on how many lines of track to use, the weight of the trains, and the approximate operating speed of the trains. These factors play an important part in bridge selection and should be calculated accurately. Too much weight or excessive speed can put a lot of stress on a bridge and eventually destroy it. Collapsing bridges may be interesting, but they are not practical.

You should also keep in mind that most narrow-gauge railways were often on the brink of bankruptcy and rarely had suitable equipment. If bridges were needed to continue their line, only the cheapest, most easily constructed bridges were built.

The terrain and location of your prototype also influences the selection of bridges. The bridge model should take advantage of its location, rather than try to overcome obstacles by brute force. Different bridge types are better for certain conditions than others, but there is no perfect bridge for each situation. This gives you an advantage over the real railroad because you can simply adjust the terrain to suit the bridge.

Bridge is the general term for a structure used to carry track over an opening. Railroad bridges are either fixed or movable. Fixed bridges are intended to be permanent. When several bridges are constructed in succession and the area to be crossed is shorter in length than in height, the structure is frequently called a *trestle*. If the distance to be crossed is greater in length than in height, the structure is referred to by modelers as a *viaduct*.

One important distinction between bridges is whether the train runs on top of the trusses, or girders (ornamental framework of a bridge), or whether it runs between them. If the train runs on top, the bridge is considered a *deck bridge*. If the train runs between the trusses, the bridge

Fig. 10-3 A good example of a simple "deck" bridge. Courtesy of National Archives.

Fig. 10-4 A truss bridge at Devil's Gate. Courtesy of Union Pacific Railroad Museum Collection; photo by William H. Jackson, 1869.

is considered a *through bridge*. Deck bridges are used when clearance under the bridge is not necessary. Through bridges do provide clearance, but they are more expensive to build and support.

FIXED BRIDGES

Beam

Beam bridges are the simplest of all bridge types, because the main components are beams of wood, steel, or concrete. Beam bridges made from wood or concrete have "floors" constructed over the supporting beams, whereas steel bridges have "open" floors. The span of beam bridges is usually short—a maximum of 16 feet for timber and 40 feet for steel and concrete. Beam bridges are also used as a framework to support the floor of other types of bridges, such as timber trestles.

Plate Girder

Plate-girder bridges can be either deck or through type. They are simply an extension of a beam bridge with larger supporting beams for greater strength. Since they are more elaborate and more expensive to build, through-type girder bridges are used only when there is insufficient clearance for a deck-type girder. Plate-girder bridges are constructed of two or more steel plates set on edge and reinforced with steel angles. This type of bridge is

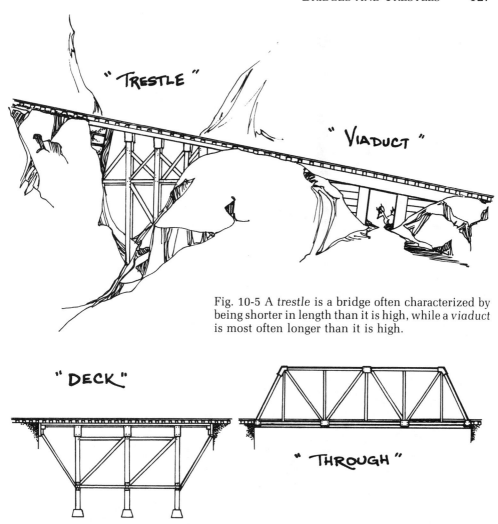

Fig. 10-5 A *trestle* is a bridge often characterized by being shorter in length than it is high, while a *viaduct* is most often longer than it is high.

Fig. 10-6 As you can tell from the illustration, a "deck" bridge runs on top of the trusses and a "through" bridge runs between them.

best for spans ranging from 15 to 100 feet, and it is often used to support the floor of truss bridges.

Truss

One of the most common bridge types is the truss bridge. These graceful, complex structures are also the most popular bridges among modelers. Truss bridges are composed of a series of different size triangles. Their

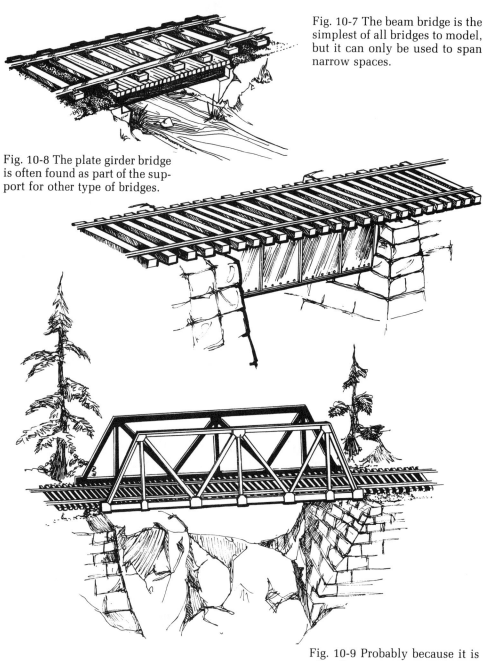

Fig. 10-7 The beam bridge is the simplest of all bridges to model, but it can only be used to span narrow spaces.

Fig. 10-8 The plate girder bridge is often found as part of the support for other type of bridges.

Fig. 10-9 Probably because it is attractive, common, and very sturdy, the truss bridge is one of the most popular bridges to model.

strength relies on the shape of a triangle, which cannot be altered without changing the length of at least one of its sides. Triangular units are fitted together in tension or compression, without bending, and the resulting structure is as strong as the material used in its construction. Truss bridges are found in both deck and through styles, and they have greater strength and support than either beam or girder-type bridges.

Arch

Arch bridges are deck-type bridges with the "arch" framework constructed under the floor of the bridge. Their load-carrying ability relies upon the compressive strength of materials, since an arch bridge thrusts outward as well as downward on its supports. Wood, stone, concrete, and steel are all suitable materials for construction.

The first stone arch bridge constructed for railroad use in the United States was for the B&O railroad in 1829. Wooden arch bridges were generally of the covered type because early timber bridges were built with untreated wood and, unless covered, had short life spans. By the turn of the century, stone and timber arch bridges were practically nonexistent because reinforced concrete had been developed. However, the concrete

Fig. 10-10 The arch bridge is among the oldest types known. In addition to the brick illustrated here, stone, timber, concrete and steel are used for their construction.

bridge never quite gained the popularity in the United States that it did in Europe, so steel arch bridges are still the most common today.

Cantilever

Cantilever bridges are larger versions of the arch bridge and are used to span large canyons and wide bodies of water, such as rivers and small bays. Although beautiful, this type of bridge is usually too long for modeling purposes. However, if you insist on modeling a cantilever bridge, see the section in this chapter on selective compression to reduce the size of the bridge for better space economy on the layout. A cantilevered bridge consists of three main components: the anchor arm (the main support of the bridge) attaches at track level and mid-distance down the embankment; the cantilever arm, the next section of bridge toward the center forms the left and right sections of the arch design; and the suspended span of the bridge (the direct center portion of the bridge), which is not supported at all but is "suspended" between the cantilever arms.

Cantilever bridges have been in existence for centuries. The first one in the United States, with three 375-foot spans, was constructed in 1876

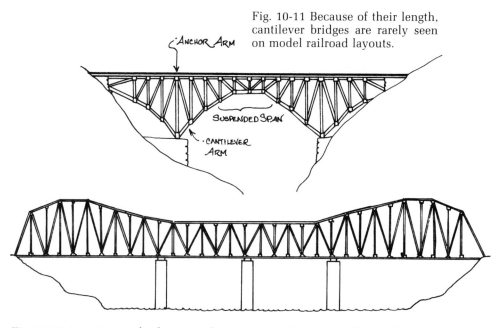

Fig. 10-11 Because of their length, cantilever bridges are rarely seen on model railroad layouts.

Fig. 10-12 A continuous bridge is another type whose length usually prohibits its inclusion in a typical layout.

over the Kentucky River for the Cincinnati Southern Railroad. A cantilevered bridge is ideal in situations where the supporting piers cannot rest on rock or other stable material, and it is much cheaper to construct than suspension bridges.

Continuous

Continuous bridges are long-span bridges built without a break over three or more supports. Because of their design, they act both as cantilevers and simple bridges. The stress factors common to cantilever bridges cancel out the stresses found in simple bridges, therefore providing a very sturdy structure. The only problem with this type of bridge is that any shifting of the pier supports places a lot of stress on the bridge, so the piers must be constructed in solid foundations.

TRESTLES

A trestle is a series of connected deck-style bridges supported on tall piers. Trestles were first constructed of wood, and they remained so until about mid-century, when steel and concrete were developed, but timber

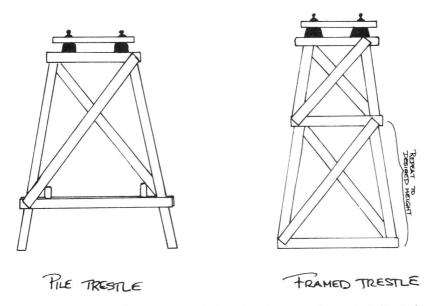

PILE TRESTLE   FRAMED TRESTLE

Fig. 10-13 Since it's built from single lengths of post, a pile trestle is limited in height. A framed trestle, being built from a series of "frames" connected together, can be of any height.

trestles are still used today. Trestle bridges can be further classified as either "pile" trestles or "framed" trestles. Pile trestles are supported by single posts driven into the ground, whereas framed trestles are supported by a series of braced uprights resting on some type of foundation. Pile trestles are limited in height, their maximum determined by the length of piles available, so they are virtually always under 25 feet high. Framed trestles, however, are practically unlimited in height. Many narrow-gauge railroads built framed trestles that were more than 100 feet high! Some trestle bridges combine pile and frame construction.

Another distinction between trestle bridges is whether the floor is "open" or "ballasted." The majority of timber trestles have open floors, but ballasted floors are necessary for high-speed lines and are used primarily for steel and concrete bridges.

Trestle bridges are also the only type generally used for bridging curved sections of track. Because of their loose framework, it is easy to design a curve into their design.

MOVABLE BRIDGES

Movable bridges are necessary when access underneath the bridge is required, generally to allow water traffic to pass, and when there is insufficient space (or money) to accommodate a fixed bridge. Movable bridges are also used as turntables or transfer tables, which transport locomotives and rolling stock to their respective roundhouses for storage. Some movable bridges are also used to connect tracks onto a barge or ferry.

Swing bridges, bascule bridges, vertical lift, and rolling bridges are

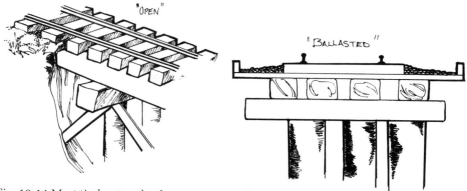

Fig. 10-14 Most timber trestles feature an open floor, but the modern steel and concrete bridges which are built for high-speed trains use a ballasted floor.

the main classifications of movable bridges, and each type engineers a different movement.

Swing

Swing bridges rotate in a horizontal plane around one or more vertical axis. Usually this axis is located in the center of the bridge, but it can be at any point, including at one end. The design of swing bridges presents no balancing problems, so the bearings needed are simple. The most common example of a swing bridge is the turntable. This type of bridge is used to switch trains from one track to another, as well as to provide access to stall tracks; it is very prototypical to narrow-gauge lines.

Swing bridges are constructed in both plate-girder and truss designs. The plate-girder swing bridges are similar to the fixed-plate girders, except that the swing bridges are heavier with extra bracing between girders to resist twisting when the bridge is not in its closed position. These plate-girder swing bridges are constructed in both deck- and through-type designs, although deck-type swings are more common. Both single and double tracks were common, and there have even been a few examples of triple-track deck plate-girder swing bridges.

Truss swing bridges were usually constructed of steel, although a few timber swings exist. This type of bridge was designed primarily to carry single lines of track. When multiple tracks were used, the trusses were connected and moved as a unit.

Bascule

Bascule bridges rotate upward around a horizontal axis. The moving section of the bridge is known as the *leaf*. If this axis is fixed in position, it is considerd a *trunnion* bridge.

Fig. 10-15 This is a good example of a truss-style, through-type multi-track swing bridge.

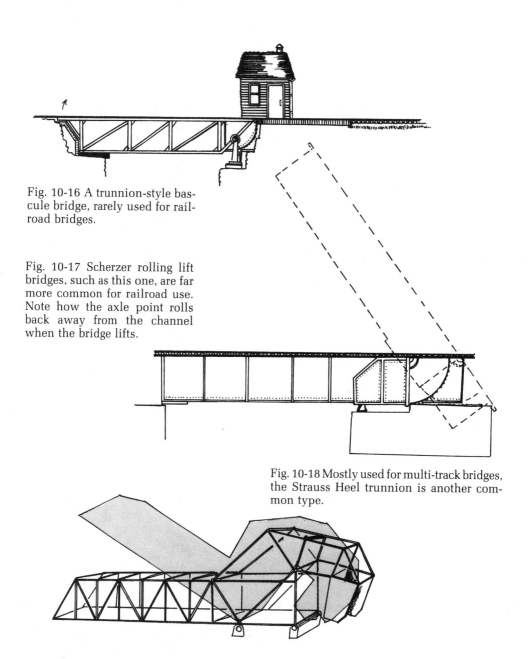

Fig. 10-16 A trunnion-style bascule bridge, rarely used for railroad bridges.

Fig. 10-17 Scherzer rolling lift bridges, such as this one, are far more common for railroad use. Note how the axle point rolls back away from the channel when the bridge lifts.

Fig. 10-18 Mostly used for multi-track bridges, the Strauss Heel trunnion is another common type.

Vertical Lift

Vertical-lift bridges practically describe themselves, opening vertically by rising like elevators. This is the most modern moving-bridge design and the only type built exclusively for railroad use. Like swing and bascule bridges, vertical lifts often served multiple track lines, although single-track vertical lifts were not uncommon. Short-span vertical lifts are plate-girder in design, and the moving section of bridge rises between four posts, one located at each corner. Larger bridges have four-post towers, often with bracing connecting the tops of the towers for added support. These bridges are usually of truss design, but some plate girders do exist.

Rolling

Rolling bridges move by rolling horizontally on rails. They require no counterweighting, so the load can be distributed over many bearings. Simple in design, this bridge was first built during the early stages of bridge development. Rolling bridges were also used for river crossings and either rolled on tracks placed at a 45-degree angle to the crossing or rolled straight back onto the bank. However, these types of rolling drawbridges are no longer in active use.

BRIDGE CONSTRUCTION

Timber Trestles

Trestles look more complicated to construct than they really are. Perhaps it is this apparent complexity that makes them such a satisfying, yet challenging, project. The most important point to remember when modeling a timber trestle is to keep the track level. And that is where we will begin construction—at track level.

The first step is to construct the open-floor framework upon which the track will be laid. Glue the track ties to the guard timbers in appropriate length for the bridge span. Proper spacing for the track ties is one tie apart. Rather than going to the trouble of trying to glue on the ties under the guard timbers, turn the whole project upside down and glue the track ties directly on top of the guard timbers. For equal spacing, you might want to make a track spacer that can be laid over the guard timbers. This will be a tremendous help for uniform spacing. When dry, turn the framework right side up and lay it on a flat, level surface. Epoxy or spike the rails to this framework. Glue both the guard rails and the running rails for added strength. You might want to weight the rails down while gluing to ensure that the trackwork stays level. Allow the glue to cure completely.

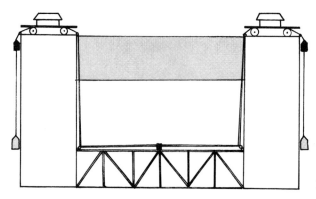

Fig. 10-19 A vertical lift bridge.

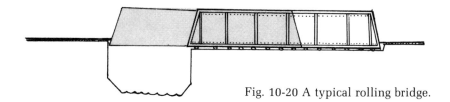

Fig. 10-20 A typical rolling bridge.

The next step is to glue stripwood of appropriate scale to the bottom of the ties for stringers and floor beams. Only a simple framework is necessary. Now you should have a flat, level floor with level track, to which the bents or piles can be added.

Prop the roadbed temporarily over the opening to be spanned and measure the distance between it and the floor below. This measurement will determine the height of the trestle bents. If the floor is not entirely level, measure at intermittant points to determine the various trestle heights needed. If the bridge is to span only a short distance, draw a full-size diagram of each of the bents and assemble them directly over the diagram.

For longer bridges, it will be worthwhile to make a simple jig. The jig will enable you to construct the bents quicker, and it will assure that each one is uniform in size.

To make a jig, you will need a flat piece of smooth-surfaced wood. On this wood piece, make a diagram of the bent with horizontal lines drawn across to indicate the various heights required. Wax paper laid over the diagram will protect the lines and prevent the wood strips from being glued to the base. Brads can be driven around the outline of the bent to hold the wood pieces in position during assembly.

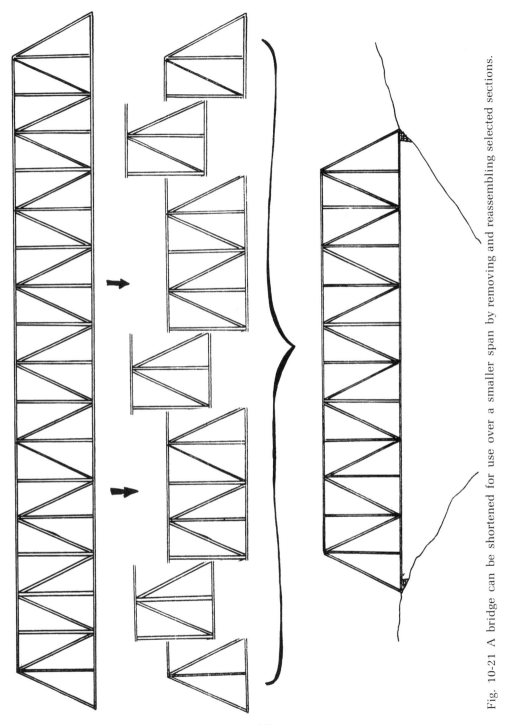

Fig. 10-21 A bridge can be shortened for use over a smaller span by removing and reassembling selected sections.

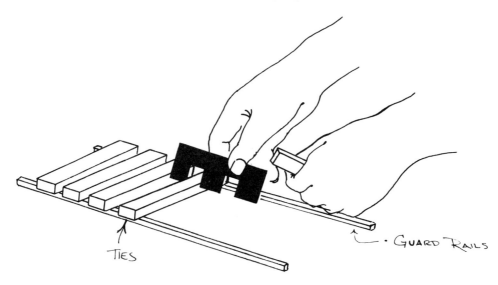

Fig. 10-22 A track-spacing tool will help to ensure uniform spacing between timbers.

Wood strips in appropriate scale should be cut to size, fitted together on the jig, and glued all at once. When all of the bents have been constructed, turn the bridge floor upside down and glue the trestle onto it. Use a machinist's square to assure that the trestle is at a perfect 90-degree angle to the floor. When dry, turn the bridge right side up and place it in position on the layout. If the track is level and the trestles are straight, glue the bridge in position. The last step is to add wood strips along the outside for girts and a few inside the bents for added bracing.

You might want to super-detail the trestle bridge for added realism. Add a refuge for pedestrians to one side of the track, at the approximate center of the bridge span. The refuge is simply a railed-in platform. Should a train happen to come along, there must be somewhere for the pedestrian to go, rather than straight down or on a free ride on the cow catcher. You might also include a red water barrel on the refuge, just in case of fire!

Swing Bridges

The swing bridge shown in Figure 10-15 is a single-track, center-bearing, asymmetrical deck plate-girder swing bridge.

Construction of this bridge is basically the same as modeling a fixed bridge, except that the framework is a little heavier. You should include the now dormant machinery to indicate that it once had worked.

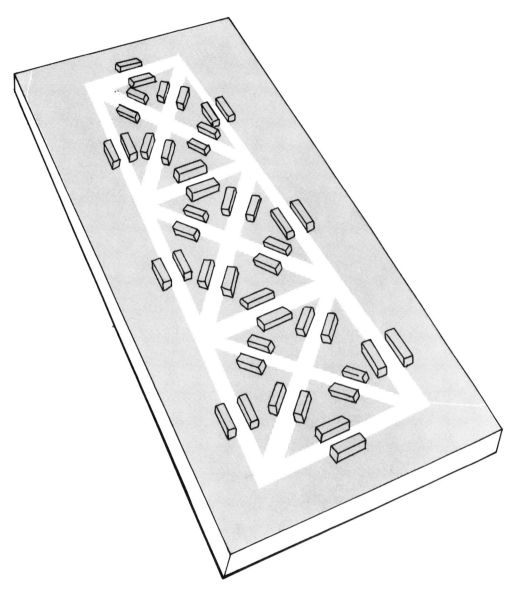

Fig. 10-23 The use of a jig can both speed up the production of bents and ensure their uniformity. The few minutes spent in its production will be quickly made up.

The first step is to construct the open-floor framework. The track ties attach directly to the plate girders, so assemble the plate girders first. Measure the opening to be spanned to determine the length of the bridge.

Now comes your first major decision: What materials are you going to use? Plate-girder bridges in real life are constructed of steel, which is not a practical modeling material. Wood is not the best choice either because the grain will spoil the look, and wood actually is not strong enough for this type of bridge. I prefer to use styrene because it is the easiest material to detail and is much stronger than wood.

Cut two pieces of styrene to the length required to span the opening. The width of the girders will depend upon the length of the bridge (the longer the span, the wider the girders need to be for adequate support), and the height of the bridge foundations. Working swing bridges are designed to move above water level at a reasonable distance, so allow at least 5 or 6 scale feet of clearance. Stringers and floor beams are also needed for plate girders, as in constructing the framework for trestle bridges. The spacing between these girders is usually about $6\frac{1}{2}$ to 7 scale feet, but this will depend upon the length of the bridge. The longer the bridge, the wider the spacing between girders.

Once the floor framework has been glued to the girders, the track ties can be glued to the tops of the girders. The track ties are wood, and they

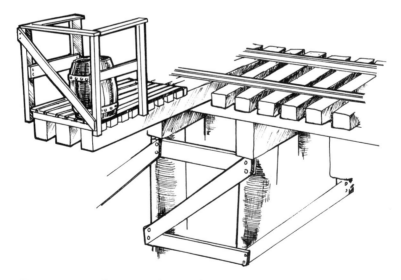

Fig. 10-24 A pedestrian refuge at the side of a bridge will add realism to your layout.

should be spaced one tie apart. Before putting the rails on, you will have to leave room on one side for a platform for pedestrians. This kind of bridge often required hand labor to move it, so a pedestrian walkway is very important. Allow approximately $2\frac{1}{2}$ to 3 scale feet for this platform. The trackwork can be laid to the other side.

The machinery will have to be realistically modeled so that it will look like it works. You will need to square strips of wood to construct the A-frame and rods. This framework will stand with one leg on one side of the track and the other leg on the opposite side of the track. You will also need some wire, just slightly smaller in diameter than coat-hanger wire, to make the rods. Leave sufficient clearance for the train to travel underneath. Cut the wood strips to length and straddle them over the trackwork. Once you have established clearance, miter the top ends and glue them together.

Use either scrap plastic or styrene to make a brace to support the A-frame and a metal cap on the tip for connecting rods. Measure the rod length; two rods will connect to the "swing" portion of the bridge on each side of the trackwork. The remaining two rods will connect to the stationary section of the bridge on each side of the trackwork. You will also need a brace to separate and support the two sets of rods. The brace should be constructed similarly to the brace supporting the wooden-beam A-frame.

This type of swing bridge was generally used for river crossings, so you may want to construct a pier foundation to support it. The pier can be built from wood scraps or from styrene strips painted to look like wood. See Chapter 11 for instructions on modeling water and embedding structures or objects in it.

Scenery

The overall weight of the layout is an important consideration when designing a model railroad. If the layout is to be set up in a permanent position, then weight is no problem. However, if you plan to display it or move it frequently, consider using lightweight scenery. There are basically two methods for producing lightweight scenery: applying a thin coating of a strong plaster over a support structure, or using a hard foam plastic such as Styrofoam.

BUILDING THE PLASTER BASE

Most lumberyards or do-it-yourself stores carry Hydrocal- or Ultracal-brand plaster. Hydrocal sets up faster and is the softer of the two in its final state, so it is easier to carve than Ultracal. However, Ultracal's longer hardening phase gives you more time to texture the surface, and since Ultracal dries harder than Hydrocal it is structurally stronger. Both materials are easy to work with.

When buying plaster, check to see that it is fresh. Old plaster will not set as quickly or be as strong as fresh plaster. Fresh plaster has a light, powdery feeling like cornstarch. Plaster that feels cakey or lumpy is too old and should be discarded.

Mixing Plaster

Both Hydrocal and Ultracal work best when mixed with an equal amount of water, and there is a simple way to do this without laborious measuring. First, use a flexible plastic bucket or bowl, which will allow

Fig. 11-1 Narrow-gauge trains often serve larger Eastern Seaboard industrial areas, so a cityscape could be an authentic addition to your layout.

you to squeeze the sides in order to remove dried, leftover plaster. Wipe a thin layer of Vaseline onto the interior surface of the bucket to make it easier to clean later. Then fill the bucket with a quantity of water about equal to the quantity of plaster you will need. Tap water is fine; water that is colder will retard the hardening process somewhat, and hot water will accelerate it.

Sprinkle a cupful of plaster into the water. This process is somewhat tedious, but it will avoid lumpiness and uneven hardening, which occur when plaster and water are mixed together haphazardly. Continue sifting until the water will absorb no more plaster and the surface looks like a desert floor, then stir. For a smooth surface, mix the plaster with your hands. First, apply a light coat of Vaseline to your hands to prevent the plaster from sticking to them.

Now you have a smooth 50–50 mixture to work with. Hydrocal will set up in 15 to 20 minutes; Ultracal will set up in about 30 minutes. You can decrease the setting time by increasing the proportion of plaster to

Fig. 11-2 Plaster scenery is the easiest and cheapest kind to install. With practice, a large area can be done in a few hours. The lighter area shows where various rock molds have been used on the Narrow Gauge Guild's new layout at the Whistle Stop in Pasadena.

water, although you will run the risk of dry spots or lumps. A better way to decrease setting time is to add a teaspoon of salt per gallon of plaster. To increase the setting time to allow you about five to ten minutes of extra work time, add a tablespoon of vinegar. For extra strength and binding capability, add a tablespoon of white glue for each gallon of plaster.

Plaster heats up as it sets. When the plaster is cool to the touch, it has set enough to begin painting. If the plaster is fully dry when you are ready to paint, simply spray the surface with water with a plastic spray bottle.

The Structural Support

Plaster needs a structure to support it. Basic scenery outlines such as mountains and ridges should be cut from Masonite or ⅛-inch plywood.

Fig. 11-3 Sprinkling plaster slowly into water until it will absorb no more will ensure a smooth, even mixture.

Mountain and valley shapes can be built up with cardboard boxes and crumpled newspapers or paper towels. Drape industrial-grade paper towels, heavy mat cloth, or loose-weave linen soaked in plaster over the shapes to form the basic scenery. Hydrocal is best for this because of its lightness. A single layer of plaster-soaked paper towels or gauze can support itself over about a 6-inch span, or use several layers for added strength. Be sure to protect the track and any other permanently placed structures from splashing plaster. Masking tape ($\frac{3}{4}$-inch wide) is perfect for covering track. Other structures can be covered with plastic wrap.

Allow each layer to dry thoroughly before applying the next. A hair dryer can be used to speed the drying time. After all of the layers are dry, remove some of the prop supports to reduce the weight. You will have to decide whether or not a structure adds enough strength to the layout to warrant its weight.

To hide the texture of the paper towels or gauze, apply a thin coat of Hydrocal. As it sets, stroke the surface with a stiff brush, following the lay of the landscape. Use the hardened pieces of Hydrocal that break off to simulate dirt and rocks.

Fig. 11-4 This shows two facets of modeling on the Narrow Gauge Guild's layout. Notice the thick (¾ inch) plywood cookie-cutter subbase for track and the layer of Homosote for sound insulation. You can also see the paper towels, which were soaked in wet plaster before installation.

Precolor the final layer of Hydrocal with a mixture of Rit dye or powdered tempera paint and plaster so that chips of white plaster won't show through. To choose the appropriate color for the plaster, find color photographs of the area you are modeling. Soil colors vary greatly from area to area. Choose a general earth tone like light brown, dark brown, or sand (a little yellow or gray added to light brown) that is appropriate to the locale. The color of the plaster will be obscured by other textures and paints, so an exact color match is not critical.

Powdered tempera paint is good for coloring plaster scenery. The liquid form of this water-based paint tends to weaken plaster, but it can be bought in powder form at Standard Brands, a nationwide chain of paint stores, and at larger fine-art stores. Mix the powder to a thin-paint consistency according to package directions in a bucket of water before adding

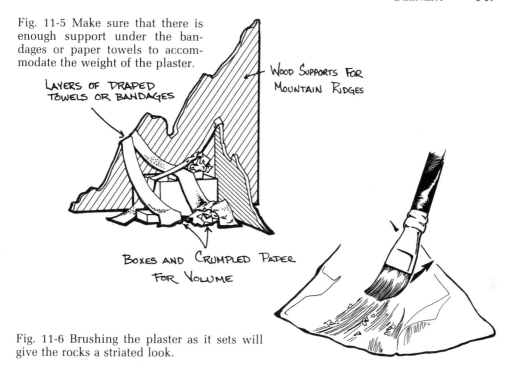

Fig. 11-5 Make sure that there is enough support under the bandages or paper towels to accommodate the weight of the plaster.

LAYERS OF DRAPED TOWELS OR BANDAGES

WOOD SUPPORTS FOR MOUNTAIN RIDGES

BOXES AND CRUMPLED PAPER FOR VOLUME

Fig. 11-6 Brushing the plaster as it sets will give the rocks a striated look.

the plaster. The plaster will lighten the color of the tempera as it dries, so experiment with small amounts of paint and plaster before mixing a bucketful. Once you have found the color you want, write down the formula in a notebook so that you can match it later. Remember that in nature the earth is not one solid color, so aim for subtle color variations for realism.

Another way to build a lightweight structure is to use fine wire screening. The aluminum metal mesh used for window screens is best and can be purchased at most hardware stores. Build wood formers like those used for the plaster structures. The mesh will support itself for about a square foot, so you won't need as much support for the plaster bandages. Fasten the mesh in place with a staple gun and cover with plaster bandages as before.

A third way to support scenery is to use a web of corrugated cardboard. Constructed properly, this kind of a structure is strong and light and the materials are inexpensive. Old cardboard boxes can usually be found for free, if you don't mind doing a little scavenging. Some supermarkets have trashbins full of empty cardboard boxes in the back that are available for the asking.

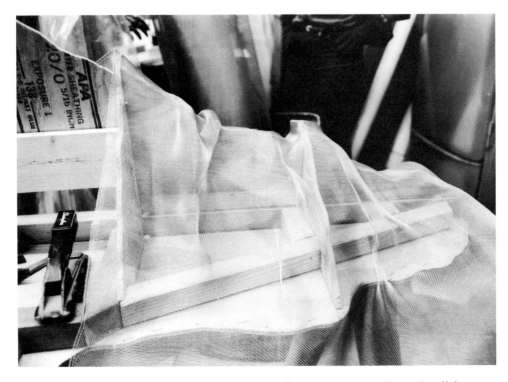

Fig. 11-7 Wire-mesh screening allows you to sculpt mountains easily and still have an adequately strong support for the plaster.

Lay the cardboard flat and use a metal ruler and matte knife to cut the cardboard into 1-inch strips. Cut the strips perpendicular to the grain of the corrugation. Start laying a web to form hill profiles. Use a staple gun, white glue and clothespins, or hot melt glue to fasten the web pieces together. Once the ridge line is formed, run formers about 6 inches apart from the ridge to the base. Bend and shape the strips to form hill and valley shapes according to your layout plan. After the formers are finished, complete the web by running strips parallel to the ridge line. The completed web should not have any open spaces larger than 6 inches. To make changes, simply cut and add strips, or push down and reglue where necessary.

To accommodate bridges, tunnel portals, or other structures into the cardboard web, simply attach cardboard wings to the structure with hot melt glue and use these wings to connect to the cardboard web. In addition to lightness and strength, this method has the advantage of leaving the entire scenery base hollow, so you have additional storage space and easy access to wiring.

Rock Molds

Rock formations can be added to your layout by carving the surface layer of plaster or, more easily, by using simple latex rock molds.

To make latex rock molds, you will need liquid latex rubber, which can be found in larger craft and hobby shops or in makeup and theatrical supply houses. You will also need some gauze, a disposable 1-inch paintbrush, and some rubbing alcohol or ammonia.

The first step is to collect some rocks with an interesting texture, such as granite, petrified wood, coal, or igneous rocks, to use as master patterns. Rocks such as sandstone that have a loose, grainy texture will not stand up well to the molding process. Wash the rock well to remove all of the loose surface dirt, then dip it in a mixture of detergent and water. The detergent (several drops to half a gallon of water) helps to break the surface tension of the water so it flows into all the nooks and crannies of the rock.

Next, brush a thin layer of latex onto the wet rock. Remove any air bubbles. This first layer of latex is the actual detail-molding surface, so you want it to be as sharply defined as possible.

Apply 5 or 6 more coats of latex. Allow each coat to dry thoroughly before applying the next coat. You can accelerate the drying process by using a hair dryer or heat gun, or you can allow the latex to air-dry overnight. For the last layer of the mold, press strips of gauze into the wet latex and brush another, thicker coat over the gauze. This reinforces the strength of the mold and makes it last longer. Clean the brush with ammonia or alcohol.

Set the mold aside for a day or two to allow it to cure completely, then remove it from the rock. Gently work one corner free, then continue to work around the edges. You must be careful not to tear the mold detail. Small bits of latex may remain embedded in the rock, but try not to tear any major chunks out of the mold. With care and patience, you will be able to separate the mold from the rock intact. Don't allow the sides of the mold to touch or they will stick together. Dust the mold with talcum powder and trim off any ragged pieces with a pair of scissors.

You may want to vary the texture of rock faces by using two or three different types of real rocks for patterns. Also, if you turn the mold slightly each time you use it, the formation will not look the same as the previous one.

The next step is to add the simulated rocks after the second layer of plaster bandages. On the layout, mark the areas to be covered and spray them with water. Wetting the surface keeps it from leaching water out of the rock castings, which could cause them to be dry and crumbly. Run

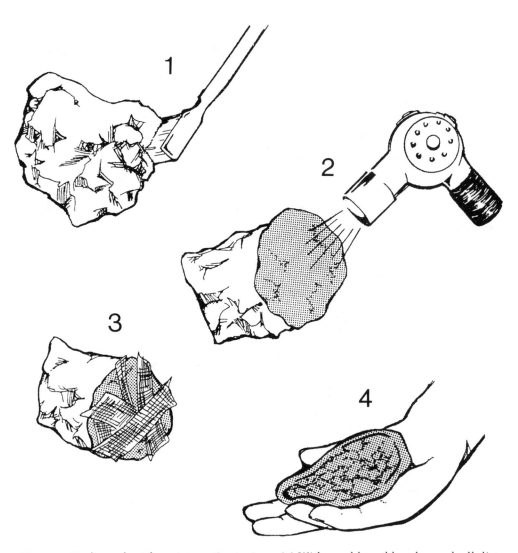

Fig. 11-8 Find a rock with an interesting texture: (1) With an old toothbrush, scrub all dirt and debris from the surface. (2) Apply five or six coats of latex, allowing each coat to dry thoroughly before applying the next. Use a blow dryer to speed drying time. (3) Embed gauze into the last layer of latex and cover completely. The gauze adds structural strength to the latex mold. (4) When the mold is dry, gently peel off the master. For convenience, the completed mold should fit comfortably into your hand.

warm water over the molds and leave the inner surface wet but not soaking. This will help the plaster flow into all the details of the mold.

Mix the plaster and coloring. When mixing coloring into plaster, it is best to use a little more plaster to keep the mix from becoming too dark. Experiment first with the proportions of coloring and plaster. Dry color pigments are concentrated, so only a small amount is needed. For example, if you are modeling granite, a mixture of $\frac{3}{4}$ teaspoon of black pigment to 2 cups of plaster will produce a nice medium gray.

The next step is to add the color variations. Black mortar can be used for the lines and darker areas. Use the color pigment to paint the surface after the plaster is dry. Before painting, note that the dark lines in granite run fairly horizontal with some vertical striation. Add the white highlights of granite by dabbing white acrylic across the surface. Quartz veins can be added by spraying thin, wet plaster into the cracks of the rocks and allowing it to dry. Granite also contains specks of orange and other colors, so dry-brush these colors last.

When painting sandstone and other stratified rocks, mix some yellow ochre in a spray bottle and spray on horizontal lines of color. In another spray bottle, mix burnt sienna and spray lines across the yellow-ochre spray. The colors will run together, giving a color variation to the surface. When dry, spray the entire surface with a dark brown so that the color runs into the cracks and crevices. Mix a little white with the yellow ochre and burnt sienna for dry-brushing highlights. To simulate erosion, trickle color down rock faces with an eyedropper.

Mix the plaster for the mold. A 50–50 mixture of Ultracal provides little grain and a good texture. To avoid air bubbles, set the mold on the floor and pour the plaster in a thin stream from waist height. The air bubbles will disperse on the way down. Now cut several 6-inch squares of toweling or mesh and press them lightly into the back of the mold. The plaster now should be thick enough so that it will no longer slosh in the mold. Starting at the highest elevation of the rock face, press the mold to the layout. Gently press down all the edges to ensure a good seal. Latex is flexible, so the mold should conform to the mountain shape. Don't worry if some plaster is forced out around the edges of the mold. We'll take care of this in a minute.

If you find that the curing time of the plaster is too slow, you can use a trick we discoverd at Movie Miniatures. Add a small amount of plaster (about 4 tablespoons) to half a gallon of water and stir. Allow it to sit for 15 to 20 minutes. Proceed to add plaster as normal and pour it into the

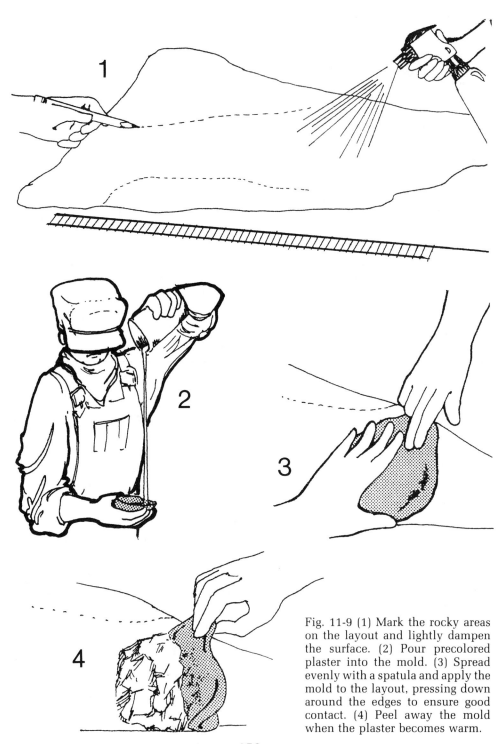

Fig. 11-9 (1) Mark the rocky areas on the layout and lightly dampen the surface. (2) Pour precolored plaster into the mold. (3) Spread evenly with a spatula and apply the mold to the layout, pressing down around the edges to ensure good contact. (4) Peel away the mold when the plaster becomes warm.

mold. Using the premixed plaster cuts the catalyzing time to 5 minutes or less. Work in assembly-line fashion:

1. Have the molds and materials ready and premix the plaster and water
2. Mix another batch of plaster
3. Add plaster to the first solution, pour it into mold, and apply
4. Repeat Steps 2 and 3 until you are finished

When the Ultracal begins to get warm, gently peel the mold away. If you leave the mold on until the plaster is hard, the mold will be trapped in the crevices and will rip where you remove it. Before the plaster completely hardens, chip away any excess with a putty knife. If you have a seam, you can scrape off the chips of plaster and use them later as loose rocks and debris. If there are gaps between the molds, you can fill them easily by tearing a piece of aluminum foil slightly larger than the gap you wish to cover, crumpling it up so that it has a similar texture to the rocks, and using it as a mold to be filled with plaster to cover the gap.

Repeat the process several times to finish a large area of rock outcropping, using fresh batches of precolored plaster each time. With practice, you can keep the plaster from becoming too thick. Leave some areas of roughened Hydrocal (added as a second layer) on the hilltops and in valleys as "dirt" to contrast with the rock texture. Stain the rocks with diluted Rit dye and add loose dirt to the horizontal faces.

If track runs close to the rock faces, you will need to put in a retaining wall, just as real railroads must use retaining walls to bolster mountain faces. You can purchase retaining walls ready-made in a variety of scales, or you can make your own from scale lumber or by carving brick or stone patterns into the plaster face of the layout. Once again, refer to your reference photographs for the appropriate placement of the walls.

LIGHTWEIGHT PLASTIC SCENERY

There are two types of hard foam plastic that can be used for lightweight scenery. Sheets of expanded polyfoam can be used to build up the mountains, or you can use two-part polyfoam plastic and catalyst liquids such as Mountains-in-Minutes.

Sheets of polyfoam can be found at industrial packing firms, and sheets of Styrofoam can be bought at most hobby or craft stores. Cut the foam into blocks and stack them on top of each other to form basic contours. Make sure to leave the blocks oversized because they will be carved down. The blocks can be glued together with either hot melt glue or white glue.

Fig. 11-10 Oversized blocks of foam can be filed down to follow predrawn contour lines.

After securely gluing the blocks together, carve and contour them with a coarse rasp, coarse sandpaper, or even with a kitchen butcher knife. To seal the texture of the foam, cover with a thin coating of Hydrocal and proceed according to the steps for making plaster scenery. The basic advantage of Styrofoam is its extremely light weight. Also, if you are planning a layout that will be moved around, the Styrofoam under the plaster will prevent the plaster from cracking in transit without adding any significant weight.

A simple, light layout can be made with a plywood subbase and with Homosote roadbed and open-grid-type benchwork. The benchwork can be made of 1 × 2 inch boards set 18 inches apart. The plastic scenery is light enough not to require heavy benchwork. When the trackwork is complete, the polyfoam sheets can be fitted into the open areas and placed beneath the tracks over bridges. Mountains left hollow will save on the material.

Mountains-in-Minutes scenery kits or industrial A-B foams (much cheaper) contain two-part polyfoam plastic and catalyst liquids. Industrial A-B foams can be bought at plastics stores. The catalyst liquids expand 15 to 30 times its volume, so a little goes a long way. Use sparingly;

Fig. 11-11 This benchwork will serve as the basis for a fishing village. Note the openings in the backboard to allow access to the model from behind.

experiment with a small amount, about an ounce of each, to find out how much area it will cover.

When mixing A-B foams, be sure to follow the printed instructions. Have plenty of paper cups and stirring sticks on hand. Be sure to get paper cups that are wax-coated. The foam will destroy plastic cups, Styrofoam cups, or plastic-coated cups. To mix the foams most efficiently, attach a power paint stirrer to a drill. Measure out equal amounts of the A and B materials in separate cups. Into a third cup pour both catalyst liquids and start stirring. The liquid will turn dark, then, as you stir it, it will turn lighter and begin to bubble. At this point, pour the rapidly expanding material over the areas you wish to cover on the layout. Do not touch the material until it has completely hardened. Wear gloves and be careful not to get this solution on your skin.

There are two ways to use A-B foam: Apply them over the carved polyfoam hills and valleys, or just pour over mountains made from wadded up newspapers and masking tape, then let them bubble and expand. Cover the paper with a slightly wet sheet of newspaper to give a smoother surface

Fig. 11-12 The mountainous terrain through which this locomotive is traveling was created with Mountains-in-Minutes.

for the foam to adhere to. To achieve the desired shapes, add more poly-foam, or carve and shape it as you did the block foam.

LANDSCAPING WITH PAPIER-MÂCHÉ

If you want your scenery to be composed of flatlands and small rolling hills, you may not want to get involved with the complexity of supporting structures for plaster or carving foam. Even flatlands are not totally smooth and level, so to provide gentle undulations to flat areas, try using Celluclay or Sculptamold, two commercial papier-mâché-like products. Mix according to the directions on the package. In addition, add 1 or 2 tablespoons of white glue to the mixture to add strength and adhesive power. Rub the

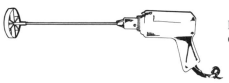

Fig. 11-13 An electric paint stirrer is the most efficient way to mix A-B foams.

Fig. 11-14 A small amount of glue added to the Celluclay mixture will increase its strength.

mixture over the surface of the layout. At first it will not stick, but continue rubbing and the mixture will smooth into an even coating. Do not plan to make hills much more than $\frac{1}{2}$-inch deep out of these preparations because they take a long time to dry, as much as 2 or 3 days.

Papier-mâché also works well as a road surface. Cut a roadbed from thin cardboard and glue it to the layout with white glue. Be sure to weight the cardboard as it dries so that it won't buckle. When the glue has dried, cover the roadbed with the papier-mâché, smoothing it over with your fingers until it becomes thin and sticky. If it starts to stick to your fingers, dip your fingers into water and continue rubbing. Potholes and wheel ruts can be added with the wooden end of a paintbrush before the papier-mâché dries. Embankments can be made simply by smoothing some of the papier-mâché along the edge of the roadway. When dry, paint and texture it like the rest of the layout.

Papier-mâché materials are also good for making crumbly, nondescript rocks. Mix the material with about a third less water than the directions call for; the mixture should be thick and puttylike. Smooth the mixture onto the layout base with a trowel, using the trowel to carve simple strat-

Fig. 11-15 Roads on a layout can be made using Celluclay or Sculpta-mold over a cardboard surface.

ifications into the material. Allow to dry. This material is good to use in places where the rock faces would be dried and worn-looking—for instance, along dry riverbeds. Color papier-mâché rocks just as you would plaster castings.

GROUNDWORK AND GROUND COVER

Now that the basic construction of the scenery is done, you can start adding realism. The most important key to this is scale. Your layout will lose its realism if the trains run past blades of grass that are as thick as a (scale) man's leg. Rather than try to model each individual blade of grass, try to cover areas with textures to achieve the best look. The use of textures is not a new concept in model railroading, but we are constantly refining the techniques to heighten the feeling of realism in films.

Fig. 11-16 The Narrow Gauge Guild layout at the Whistle Stop has many different kinds of scenic treatments. Notice the wood retaining walls and rubble, and the small lateral space between tracks.

Dirt

Now that the rocks are in place, the next layer to be added is ground dirt. It always amazes me that people spend so much time and money to find things to simulate plain old dirt. Now, I'm not saying to go grab a handful from your garden and dump it on your layout; but with a little care you can make ordinary dirt look just like ordinary dirt.

To prepare the dirt, you will need a bucket, a small shovel, a collander and hand-sifter, a pair of nylon stockings, and several containers, such as plastic margarine containers. The plastic lids keep everything snuggly in place. Most people seem to have a few rattling around in the back of their cupboards, and they are easy to come by. You can even ask friends to save them for you.

The first thing to do is to take the bucket and a shovel and go collect some dirt. Choose a time when the ground is dry, so you won't wind up with clumps of soil. If the ground is wet, spread dirt onto a cookie sheet and place it in the oven (not the microwave) at a low temperature to dry. Scrape away the top layer of ground cover, since this will be mostly leaves and twigs too large to use. Once you get to the earth level, try to scoop your earth from the top 6 inches of ground. This is where the dirt is the loosest, and you can avoid rocks.

Take the dirt home and, starting with a collander, sift it. Sift into an old newspaper so that you can use the crease of the paper to funnel the dirt into containers. Take the chunks left in the strainer and put them in a container. Small rocks and twigs can be used later as boulders and tree trunks, but bits of grass and leaves are not useful and can be discarded. Resift the dirt on the paper with the hand-sifter and set aside the remains. The last sifting is through the nylon stockings, which will yield a fine-grained dirt very much like talcum powder. This is the most desirable texture, and you will wind up with one-half to three-quarters of the original amount, depending upon the dirt in your area, so make sure that you gather enough.

Latex paint is the binder most commonly used by model railroaders. A soft, warm brown is a good base color, but the color you choose will depend on your prototype. Use photos for reference. Test colors by diluting a small amount of modeler's acrylics (like Polly S) 50-50 with water and paint some test swatches on an inconspicuous area of the layout. Once you've found a color that you like, take the bottle to your local Standard Brands, Sears, or other paint store and try to match the paint chips. You'll want flat acrylic latex wall paint. If you can't find a standard color that you like, check the custom-mix color chart. You will be thinning this latex paint with water, so keep this in mind when figuring how much to buy. Many paint companies sell empty paint cans. If you buy one and put your paint into it, you may be able to persuade them to put it on their paint mixer for you.

Brush the paint generously onto the scenery base so that it will flow into all of the cracks and crevices. Paint an area about one foot square, then apply texture and repeat until you have covered the entire layout. If the paint seems to be drying too fast, wet the area before applying paint. Any areas where the texture doesn't take can be repainted.

The texture can be applied in a number of ways. Some modelers use small jars with holes poked in the lid. I use a hand-strainer (like a baby-food strainer) held about two feet above the base to get thin, even coverage.

Before the paint has time to dry, apply the bonding agent. Use an eyedropper on small areas and a basting syringe for large ones. For a bonding agent, use a thinned mixture of artist's matte medium and water with just one or two drops of detergent. This can be sprayed on, but you must be sure to soak the area thoroughly. This phase will go quickly, and you will be rewarded with a layout that appears to be finished.

Just as a note, some modelers prefer to use white glue to apply the initial ground cover. Diluted 1:3 with water, white glue provides adequate

Fig. 11-17 Apply paint generously to the scenery base. Be sure that the paint is thin enough to flow easily into cracks and crevices.

Fig. 11-18 Baby-food jars with holes poked in the lid are a simple way to apply ground cover over the wet paint.

stickiness, but it can dry with an objectionable shine, and it doesn't give the overall earth tone that the latex paint provides.

Let the groundwork dry overnight. This gives the bonding medium a chance to cure. Brush away any loose groundwork and decide if bare spots need to be reapplied or whether they will be covered by other things later. If you want to vacuum up the loose texture material, place a piece of cloth over the tip of a vacuum so that you can save the material for use later.

I prefer to spray on color rather than brush it on. Here is where an airbrush is ideal, but if you don't have one, a spray bottle will do. For the next step, mix a thin black wash of artist's acrylic, water, and a few drops of detergent. Mars Black is a "warm" black made from a red-base pigment. Ivory Black is mixed from a blue pigment, so it is "cooler." Mars Black is good for overall washes, whereas Ivory Black is best for shadows on rock faces and waterfalls.

Spray the diluted pigment over the entire layout. Make sure that the spray is fairly heavy so that the pigment soaks the texturing material. When dry, the black will stay in the areas between each dirt granule, highlighting the shadows. Spray a heavier coat where rock faces cast shadows or on other areas where natural shadows would occur. Also spray the rock faces and allow them to dry completely.

Fig. 11-19 If you don't have an airbrush, use a spray bottle to apply washes to the ground-work, but make sure that the paint mixture is very thin to prevent clogging the nozzle.

The next step is to dry-brush highlights over all surfaces. Dry-brushing will lighten the color of the layout and bring out texture and detail. Once again, you will have to refer to photos, but a combination of warm browns and yellows is appropriate for highlighting. Burnt sienna, yellow ochre, and raw umber work well for almost any type of landscape. Usually I will start with raw umber, since it is the darkest.

Dry-brushing consists of flicking small amounts of paint over the raised surfaces of the texture. You can achieve this by picking up a small amount of paint on the tips of the brush bristles and lightly wiping them over the surface. If you apply too much paint, wipe off the excess with a towel. After a little practice, you will find this technique comes easily.

A stiff chisel-tipped brush works better than a pointed one, and fan-tipped brushes, sold by some art stores, work even better. The paint should be very dry. I usually use it straight from the tube without any water added. Make two or three dry brush passes over the entire layout, each time using a lighter color. Use the darker colors along river beds and in valleys and the warm red of burnt sienna along hill ridges and other areas that catch the sun. The yellow ochre will be the lightest highlight.

It is always easy to change an area that you don't like simply by dry-brushing over the dry paint and, if necessary, respraying with black wash.

Fig. 11-20 When dry-brushing highlights onto scenery, wipe all but a small amount of paint off the brush and run it lightly over the surfaces to paint the high points.

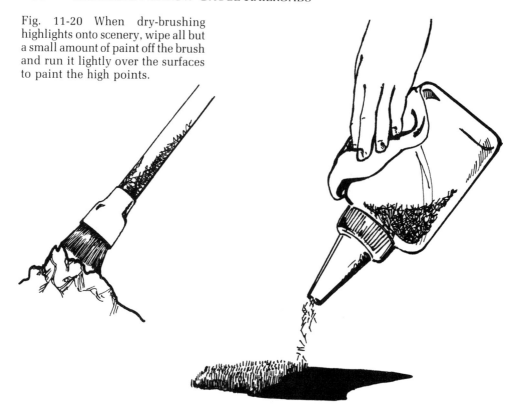

Fig. 11-21 When using electrostatic grass, first rub the bottle with a dry cloth to build up a static charge; then squeeze the grass onto the wet paint of the groundwork.

Grass

In some areas, you may want the ground cover to be grass rather than dirt. Instead of sifting dirt over the wet latex paint, use an electrostatic applicator (a small plastic squeeze bottle) to apply electrostatic grass. Electrostatic grass is made up of many tiny hairlike fibers of acrylic, and it can be bought at most well-supplied hobby stores. When the squeeze bottle is held three to six inches above the freshly painted surface, the electric charge between the bottle and paint causes the fibers to stand on end once they are squeezed from the bottle.

If you decide to apply the grass after you have already laid down the dirt and painted it, spray the area with diluted white glue or acrylic matte medium. Once the adhesive has dried, the electrostatic grass can be air-brushed, but I don't recommend dry-brushing it. Some modelers like to use sawdust as grass, but to me it always looks like sawdust. Ground foam is an acceptable coarser foliage, which can be purchased in a variety of colors at most hobby stores. Woodland Scenics makes a good product. The foam is also applied over a wet adhesive and can be similarly airbrushed and dry-brushed.

Flocked paper grass, which can be bought at most large hobby stores, is an easy way to cover large areas. Bury the edges of the paper in finely sifted dirt or ground foam. Use spray adhesive to attach the grass paper to the layout.

Rocks

The next layer of ground cover includes rock rubble, bushes, and trees. For rock rubble, simply take the plaster scraps left from the rock castings and build piles of rocks where you want them. Once the piles are in place, soak them with diluted matte medium and allow them to dry. To paint, spray and dry-brush as you did the ground texture. You may want to sprinkle some dirt or grass around the edges of the pile for added realism.

Trees and Bushes

Trees and bushes can make or break the realistic look of a layout. There are a number of ways to make good-looking trees. Remember that you will need a large number of trees, but only the ones in the very front need to be highly detailed. Woodland Scenics sells cast-metal tree arma-tures that look good but are expensive. You may want to use one or two of these in the foreground and something less expensive for the main body of the foliage.

Small twigs and large weeds make good tree trunks. When gathering them, keep in mind the scale you want to achieve. Gently remove the leaves and dry the stems by spreading them on a cookie sheet and putting them in the oven at a low temperature (250°F) for an hour. Once the tree bases are dry, embed a nail in the trunk bottom and stand them in a block of Styrofoam with two or three inches of space between. Spray a base color over the trunks. A warm, medium brown works well for most types of trees. Some species of trees, such as birch or ash, may require a light gray-brown base color. Allow the base color to dry, then spray it with a dark wash. Remember to vary the shapes and sizes of trees, because in nature no two trees look exactly alike.

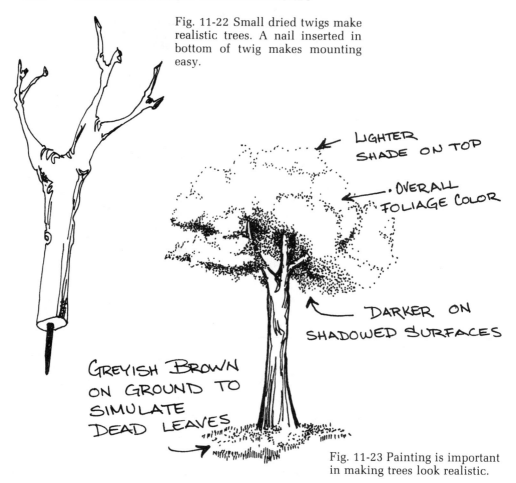

Fig. 11-22 Small dried twigs make realistic trees. A nail inserted in bottom of twig makes mounting easy.

LIGHTER SHADE ON TOP

OVERALL FOLIAGE COLOR

DARKER ON SHADOWED SURFACES

GREYISH BROWN ON GROUND TO SIMULATE DEAD LEAVES

Fig. 11-23 Painting is important in making trees look realistic.

Tree trunks can also be made from twisted wire. This method is more time-consuming than using twigs, but it produces a realistic effect. Some modelers use braided picture wire, but the kinks and twists of the wire produce unrealistically kinky branches. I prefer to buy fine wire and twist it myself. First, cut several strands of fine-gauge (18-24) wire about 6 feet long. This will be enough to make 10 or 12 trees.

Take one end of the wires and wrap them around a doorknob. Twist together the last inch and a half of the other ends of the wires and insert them into the chuck of a power drill. Back away from the doorknob until the stretched wire is under light pressure. Activate the drill at low speed. The wire will twist around itself. Stop when the wire starts to kink. Loosen

Fig. 11-24 When twisting wire with a drill, make sure that the wire is securely chucked. Then twist slowly until the wire begins to kink.

Fig. 11-26 A tapered-stake tree.

Fig. 11-25 A twisted-wire tree made from seven strands of wire. Leave a few loose wires to simulate tree roots.

the wire around the doorknob first. Cut the twisted hank of wire into tree-height lengths, 10- to 30-foot scale height. Cutting them in different lengths adds to the realism.

Make the branches by untwisting the top of the wire. Start branches about 4 scale feet above the ground level. Remember to leave enough wire to stick through the floor of the layout. Leave a few strands showing above the base of the layout to simulate exposed root systems. Thicker trees can be made by twisting more wires together. Coat the twisted wire trunk with solder, epoxy, plaster, or oven-curing clay. Paint as described in Chapter 13.

Redwood stakes can also be carved to form tree trunks, especially for modeling tall, columnar trees like poplars and pines. Another useful item for constructing trees is caspia, which can be found in the wild or purchased at florists or nurseries.

Greenery is difficult to model accurately. Joyce Kilmer once said, "Only God can make a tree," and it's *almost* true. Since lichen is not as readily available to westerners as it is to some modelers in the East, I use steel wool to form the foliage. Steel wool is available in a variety of grades at most hardware stores. Choose a grade to match the scale of the railroad.

Tear off an appropriate size chunk of steel wool and spread the fibers, pulling the wool apart until it resembles foliage. When you are satisfied with the shape, put a dab of rubber cement on the tops of each branch and glue the wool onto the tree trunk. Allow it to dry. Mask the trunk with masking tape, give the foliage a heavy coat of spray adhesive, and roll it in ground green foam. Continue to apply layers of spray, glue, and foam until you are satisifed with the look of the tree. On the final layer of foam, sprinkle a darker color foam on the underside of the tree and a slightly lighter one on the top. A note of caution: Do not allow slivers of the steel wool to attach to the motor or it will short circuit. For areas around the motors, use scouring pads as the bases for the foliage.

Woodland Scenics produces a foliage material that is made of fibers and polyurethane foam ready to use from the package. This material is very easy to use. All you have to do is take it out of the package and stretch it so that it has a see-through look. Then cut the material with scissors and drape it over the tree armatures. Dab some spots of adhesive onto the armature to hold the material in place and trim if necessary. The tree is now ready to be installed.

Lichen has been an old standby for tree making for many years. The main problem with lichen is its heavy structure, which must be camouflaged if it is to look to scale. Give the lichen a light coating of ground foam held in place with spray adhesive. I prefer the steel-wool method for foreground trees, but lichen works well to simulate background forests and distant brush-covered hillsides. One way to make a forest without making all the tree trunks is to suspend a piece of wire mesh on supports at mid-tree height. Then place a few completed trees between this support and the viewer. Cover the mesh with treetops and it will look like a complete forest. Make the treetops that will be furthest from the viewer progressively smaller than those in the immediate foreground. This will add the illusion known as forced perspective.

Consult reference photographs before placing the trees in the landscape. Trees usually look more balanced if they are placed in groups of three or more; rarely do you find a singular tree in the middle of an

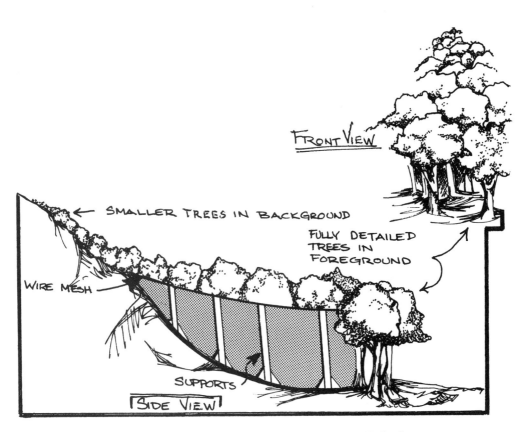

Fig. 11-27 The rear part of a forest doesn't always have to be fully built.

otherwise barren field. Once the trees are in place, go back under the foliage with some gray-brown ground foam to simulate dead leaves.

Bushes and underbrush can be made to look like treetops without the trunks. For variety, you can use areas of spagnum moss or other small bits of weed culled when picking branches. The seed tips of foxtails are made up of individual strands, and these can be pulled free with tweezers and planted in the landscape as weed clumps. Cattails and barley grass have a similar structure to foxtails and can also be used. Plant the fibers in puddles of bonding agent. Asparagus fern, available at most florist's shops, makes a good leafy bush and also works well as foliage for treetops. Baby's breath, also available at florist's shops, is another good choice. There are

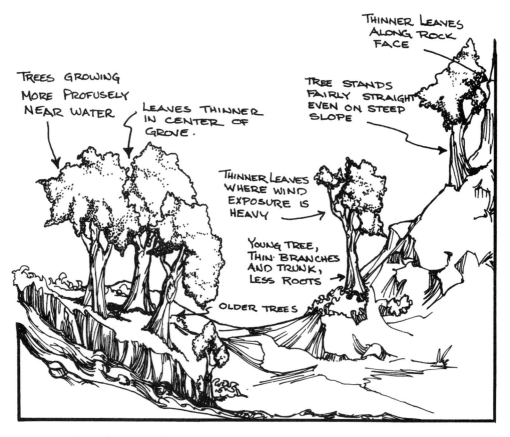

Fig. 11-28 Tree placement should follow natural patterns as much as possible.

many natural materials that can be used as foliage and brush. With time, you will develop a habit of noticing items for future reference.

If you want to use foliage from the wild, you will probably want to preserve it before painting. The most common preservative used by model railroaders is glycerin, a skin emolient that can be purchased at most drugstores. Mix the glycerin in a pot of water (1:3 ratio) with one aspirin per gallon of water. Bring the pot to near boiling and drop the foliage in the pot. Simmer for five to ten minutes, then remove from heat. When cool, scoop out the foliage and squeeze out the liquid. (If the foliage cannot be squeezed easily, simply allow it to drip dry.) Allow everything to dry completely. Once dry, the foliage is ready to paint.

You may choose to dye the foliage rather than paint it. Conventional fabric dyes such as Rit work well. Follow the directions on the package, and never mix brands of dyes. Remember that the color of the dyed item will turn several shades lighter as it dries.

Besides real plants, other items make good foliage. Untwisted hemp

Fig. 11-29 Small twigs with ground foam "leaves" make good scale trees.

Fig. 11-30A Yarrow, which is readily available from most large plant stores, makes an excellent basis for trees. Start by cutting off some small branches 6 to 9 inches in length.

Fig. 11-30B Wrap the base of the twigs with tape to produce the trunk.

Fig. 11-30C Spread out the branches to give the tree more body.

Fig. 11-30D Spray paint the upper branches with a flat, medium green enamel.

Fig. 11-30E The trunk can then be brush-painted with a flat dark brown. Here we used Tamiya's flat brown.

Fig. 11-30F The next step is to spray the branches with thinned-down artist's matte medium. A spray bottle is valuable.

173

Fig. 11-30G Sprinkle one of the medium-color grasses from Woodland Scenics onto the top edges of the branches.

11-30H Now turn the tree over and sprinkle one of the darker colored grasses onto the bottom. This simulates the darker colors of undersides of the leaves and branches.

174

Fig. 11-30I Finish off by sprinkling a very light color over the upper areas of the tree, simulating light reflecting off the leaves.

Fig. 11-30J The finished product is an excellent reproduction of a tree.

Fig. 11-31 One of the secrets of making realistic logs is to pick straight twigs with fine-grained bark. Licorice root works well to simulate old sugar pines. Use a razor saw and cut partway through the twig from both sides. Snap through the last ⅛ inch to make it appear as though the tree was felled by a logger.

175

rope will make tall, fibrous plants like swamp grass or wheat. Polypro-pylene twine, available at craft supply stores for macramé, is good for making twigs and grasses. Wool fluff, combed from felt with a wire brush, is available in a variety of colors. Form the clumps of fibers loosely into balls, or gather the clumps in piles to create thicket areas. Spray with bonding agent for adhesion. Sprinkle ground foam over the twiglike struc-tures for leaves.

To make vines, run a line of white glue with a toothpick over the wall or whatever the vine will cover. Sprinkle ground foam into the glue before it dries and blow away any excess foam. Put a twig at the bottom of the vine to simulate the stem. If you want the vines to drape over a rock or wall, dip a toothpick into the water-based contact cement and lift out the strings of glue to drape over the scenery. You may have to expose the contact cement to air for a few minutes to thicken it before it will produce strings that are sturdy enough. Immediately cover with ground foam.

MODELING WATER

Water can be an exciting visual addition to any layout, or it can be a disaster. Fortunately, there are now several good methods for modeling water. And there are products on the market that look so much like water that you have to touch them to believe they aren't real.

There are several factors that will decide what method you should use to model water. These factors include the intended weight of the layout, the depth of the water to be modeled, and whether or not the layout is movable.

For my modular layout, it was necessary to create an illusion of deep water without adding excessive weight. I decided that I had two choices of materials for simulating the water portion of the harbor. My first choice was to use rippled Plexiglas; my second choice was to pour resin.

Rippled Plexiglas

Rippled Plexiglas is an easy and fast way to model water of any depth. It can be bought at a plastics store or at large hardware stores. You can paint the top, rippled surface of the Plexiglas just as if it were plywood or Masonite and install it. I prefer to turn the rippled surface down and paint the underneath surface with various blues, greens, and grays. On the top flat surface use artist's gloss medium and build up ripples and waves. Artist's gloss medium is similar to the matte medium that we have been using as an adhesive. It is a thick, white, sticky mixture that dries with a

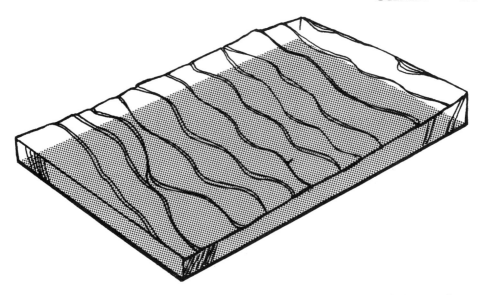

Fig. 11-32 Painting the underside of clear rippled Plexiglas allows light to reflect through for realistic water effects.

hard, shiny, clear surface. The medium has a good deal of body to it, so it can be worked into ripples while wet and then allowed to dry.

Experiment on a scrap of Plexiglas before you start on the main body of water. By building up successive layers of gloss medium, allowing each to dry before applying the next, you will find that you can create waves, ripples, and boat wakes easily. You can add a small amount of cobalt blue acrylic to the medium. When dry, this color will show only where the medium is very thick, giving just a hint of blue to waves and currents. To model the frothy look of the crests of waves, mix acrylic modeling paste with the gloss medium. Acrylic modeling paste by itself will dry pure white. It can be used on its own to build up waves and then be painted over with gloss medium and acrylic paint.

Rippled Plexiglas can also be used as a clear window over a sculptured water bottom. However, the problem with this technique is that the water surface cannot be penetrated by weeds and rocks, so it tends to look like a piece of glass over rocks and weeds. This is the main problem with using Plexiglas to simulate water: Anything that breaks the water surface must be cut at the water line, or a hole must be cut in the Plexiglas water.

No matter how you decide to use the Plexiglas, the water base must be finished before it can be placed. If you will be able to see through it, paint and apply textured rocks and weeds to the water bed as you have done to the rest of the landscape. Set the Plexiglas in place over the finished water bed and hide the edges with sand or foliage.

Polyester Resin

Using Plexiglas means that you must do a good deal of the landscaping before modeling the water. This was not practical for my tightly knit, somewhat complicated modular layout, so I decided to use poured resin, which can be applied almost last to simulate the water. There are two types of products on the market that produce excellent water surfaces. They are epoxies and polyester resins. Epoxies are generally two-part materials intended for making thick, high-gloss finishes on decoupage projects. They make very good calm water, but it is difficult to model ripples and waves. So to simulate the movement of water in a harbor, I use polyester resin.

Warning: Polyester resins smell terrible, and the fumes can be toxic and flammable. Always use them in a well-ventilated area, be sure to wear rubber gloves and an eye shield, and keep them out of the reach of children.

To prepare the scenery base for poured "water," first seal the area to form a basin. Do the rest of the landscaping and texturing first, leaving the area to be covered with water bare. Sand the water bed smooth and coat with a sealer. Use either full-strength matte medium for sealer or unthinned latex paint. Whichever medium you decide to use for sealer, try to leave as few brush marks as possible. Allow the sealer to dry thoroughly (two or three days if possible) before proceeding.

The next step is to paint the water bed. You can simulate great depth or allow it to look shallow. To simulate depth, paint the center areas black and work the earth colors from the banks down into the black, blending the colors where they meet. This is an especially easy task if you use an airbrush.

If you plan to have overhanging banks of water, now is the time to construct them. Use one of the papier-mâché mixtures for realism. Allow the papier-mâché to dry, then paint it. If you want to apply any sand or texture, thoroughly soak it with the bonding medium. It is important that any texture that will be covered by the water be firmly attached because any loose particles will create air bubbles in the poured resin and destroy the scale look. Glue in place any weeds, logs, or other detail (such as ships and piers) that are to be embedded in the water.

Allow everything to dry for several days before pouring the resin.

Follow the directions on the package for mixing the resin and hardener. Use a measuring cup with one-ounce gradations to ensure accurate measurement. If you don't measure the exact quantities, you cannot be sure of the results. Don't attempt to pour the entire body of water at once. Instead, pour it in layers about ⅛ inch deep.

Refer to the package directions to calculate how much resin to mix for each area to be covered. Mix the resin and catalyst in a disposable container. Stir gently, and be sure to scrape the sides of the container so that you get an even mixture. Try to avoid trapping air bubbles in the mix. Resin can be colored with resin dye, and now is the time to do so. When the resin is thoroughly mixed (about two or three minutes), slowly pour it into the water area. If possible, tip the layout to distribute the resin evenly. Otherwise, spread the resin to the edges with a stirring stick. Prick out any air bubbles with a toothpick or needle.

Check the resin periodically to make sure that it is setting properly. It is important that the temperature of the area surrounding the resin be

Fig. 11-33 When creating deep water with resin, pour it in a series of ⅛-inch-deep layers. Allow each layer to dry before applying the next.

at least 70 degrees, if not warmer. If the area is too cool, the resin will not cure. If you think the area might be too cool, place a pair of 100-watt bulbs above the poured resin until it starts to set. The curing process has started when you can prick the surface and it has a thick, sticky consistency. Try to keep any dust from falling onto the water surface while it is curing. If you want the surface of the water to be rippled or windblown, roughen the top layer of the resin with a stirring stick while it is curing. To accelerate the curing process, you can use a hair dryer.

Another way to model choppy water is to pour a thin surface layer of overcatalyzed resin (about 6 drops catalyst to half an ounce of resin). Stipple the surface with an old paintbrush while applying heat. Once the resin starts to stiffen, pick out any trapped air bubbles. Be very cautious when using overcatalyzed resin. If it is put on too thick, that layer will warp and crack. Experiment before applying it to the layout.

There are a few other tricks to modeling water. If you are planning to model deep water (more than $1\frac{1}{2}$ inches), rather than pour that much depth of resin, pour all but the top inch in plaster. Paint the top of the plaster deep blue, then dye each layer of resin a successively lighter shade of blue until the surface layer is clear. If you want to simulate calm, smooth water and don't have room in the layout to allow for a deep area to pour resin, paint layers of clear gloss varnish over a flat water area. Allow each coat to dry thoroughly before applying the next. For small puddles, five-minute epoxy is an easy medium to use, but be warned that it will yellow with time.

BACKDROPS AND SKYSCAPES

Although this is one of the last subjects we are going to cover on scenery, the type of backdrop should be one of the first things to consider building for the layout. You need to decide whether you want just a simple blue-sky backdrop or something more complex, such as painted hills or a printed city scene. Obviously the size of the layout will help to determine the type of backdrop you will need. No matter what size layout you have planned, a simple sky backdrop with gentle horizon detail will help to extend the three-dimensional illusion of reality.

Since most large layouts are nonportable, you can construct a permanent backdrop. Whether the planned layout is city or country, a blue or gray-blue sky is necessary. For a room-size layout, you will need a continuous backdrop. Obviously, any hard corners (such as room corners) will destroy the illusion of reality. If the layout contacts the walls of the room only on one side, you can just paint the wall. However, if it contacts two or more sides, lay down a single background surface. Most model railroaders use linoleum runners for this purpose. These can be bought in the floor-covering department of most major department stores in 36-inch widths. To support the linoleum, you will have to build a wooden framework of 1 × 3s and nail the linoleum to them. Check the plans of your house and consult with a building supply store expert to determine what supplies you will need.

The simplest way to paint a backdrop is to simulate sky. Go to a paint store for color chips of various light sky-blue paints. Compare the color chips under the lighting in which the layout will be viewed and choose the one that looks best. A sky background will look most realistic if it is blue at the top, fading down to whitish blue-gray at horizon level. Spray, brush, or roll on the latex paint, whichever you are most comfortable with.

Clouds look most realistic if they are spray painted. Consult reference photographs before starting. If you do not feel confident about painting clouds, don't. My dictum about details on a backdrop is: "If in doubt, leave it out!" Remember that the background will simply add an illusion of reality; it should not be so elaborate as to distract attention from the layout.

Sky scenery is fine for a simple background, but trees, forests, or even painted buildings can turn a 5 × 8-foot section of scenery into miles of city or countryside. Let's start with painting hills and trees and work our way up.

Follow the steps for painting a blue-sky background and let it dry completely. For best results, use watercolors to paint scenery on the backdrop. Watercolors are pale, translucent colors that allow you to build up intensity slowly without fear of creating shades that are too bright or dark. To simulate distant hills, use a pale violet or blue-gray wash. Paint wavy hill shapes at about the center of the backdrop, stretching them from one side of the backdrop to the other. Next, add green for the closer hills and trees. If you want to include a lake or structures, leave the designated areas unpainted. The greens you choose will vary in shade, reflecting the variety of colors found in nature. Paint hill shapes with light to medium shades of green, varying the colors for field or meadow areas. Dab on darker green where trees will be, or use a sponge for a textured look. If you want a few rock faces, use Polly-S Reefer White straight from the bottle to outline edges, shadows, and cracks. When dry, dry-brush light tans or grays over the rock for shadows.

Darker colors in the foreground will hide shadows cast on the backdrop by objects on the layout, and they will make the lighter areas of the backdrop seem farther away. Add yellow highlights to the tops of trees near the horizon where the sun may brighten them. If a lake is included in the scenery, paint light green reflections on the surface edges to create a mirror image of shoreline trees. Buildings on a backdrop look best if painted in the middle ground, or at the rear of the scenery. This will eliminate heavy detailing and will not distort the perspective.

Buildings

Buildings add life and realism to a model railroad, and at least one should be included on every layout. Narrow-gauge train lines center around industrial and agricultural areas, so buildings are a must. When selecting structures, keep in mind two things: the time period you want to re-create and the purpose of the narrow-gauge train. Both of these factors are interrelated and of great importance for realism.

Narrow-gauge railroads usually transported raw materials from mining, logging, and agricultural areas to industrial mills and factories. Most trains served only one industry, so all buildings included on the layout should be compatible with that particular industry. Obviously, a farmhouse plantation complete with horses and cows will look out of place near a coal-mining community.

The time period is also important when selecting structures, for it will dictate architectural style and the type of building components used. Your choice of structures can be made easier if you select buildings whose designs are neither very old nor very modern. From 1880 through 1940, most buildings were constructed from brick or stone, and they were often similar in design. If you cannot decide upon a specific era, keep all structures within this simple, timeless style. Newer buildings lack the character and run-down look necessary for a narrow-gauge railroad.

Before deciding what kind of buildings to include on the layout, go out and look at some actual buildings. Often a building may have the proper shape and design but will be too large to fit the size of your layout. Most larger buildings tend to look unrealistic and out of scale, especially on a narrow-gauge line.

Fig. 12-1 These buildings are being prepared for a commercial at Movie Miniatures and are perfect examples of the timeless style of buildings built between 1880 and 1940.

SELECTIVE COMPRESSION

Large, interesting buildings can be reduced to a suitable size for a model railroad without losing their proportions or character. This technique is known as selective compression. Selective compression does not reduce the size of the doors or windows; it merely decreases the overall dimensions of a building. The simplest method of selective compression is to reduce the number of floors of a particular structure (obviously buildings that in real life are more than two stories tall). Buildings more than three stories high tend to look out of place and out of scale, unless you are re-creating a city scene. This would be a rare exception though, since

Fig. 12-2 Another trick used by professional modelers is to make a scale model of the scale model! This model, ⅛ inch to the foot, was built in an hour to test camera angles for a science-fiction film being shot at Brick Price's Wonderworks.

most narrow-gauge train lines served mining and logging camps and often traveled through virtually inaccessible areas devoid of civilization.

Many larger structures have a basic window design that has been repeated on each floor for ease of construction. Large factories constructed from a basic shell of brick or wood often have a series of windows that span both sides of the building; these windows are all the same size and shape and spaced equally apart. By decreasing the number of windows across yet retaining their equal spacing, you can decrease the size of a prototype structure without changing its character.

For example, assume that in real life a two-story lumber mill with a loft measures 21 feet wide × 37 feet long × 28 feet high. There are five

185

Fig. 12-3A Cardboard mockups of scenery details can save a lot of grief and misspent time. It's better to plan a building for a given space than to build the structure and then try to fit it into available space.

Fig. 12-3B Cardboard mockups can be made from Xeroxes of the kit plans or even by Xeroxing the building parts. This part of modeling can be just as much fun as the finished work.

Fig. 12-4 The area under this proposed structure will have to be built up or cut into the mountain. Careful planning can save time and money, and produce an attractive layout. Note the plan drawing of the bridge, which is to go into the gap below.

windows across each side of the building per floor, giving a total of ten windows each side. When the actual measurements of this building are converted to scale, the size may not be enormous, but it might take up too much space on the layout. By decreasing the number of windows across from five to four, the length of the lumber mill can be reduced to 29 feet. This small reduction in size may seem insignificant, but when converted to scale it can make inches of difference. Use discretion when selectively compressing a building. The technique works well, but don't get carried away decreasing floors and window patterns or the character of the building will be lost.

BUILDING PLACEMENT

Plan the placement of buildings before putting the layout scenery in place. This will prevent problems later when you might discover that an industrial factory would look nice where you have planted an endless forest of evergreens. Buildings of course can be added later if you decide

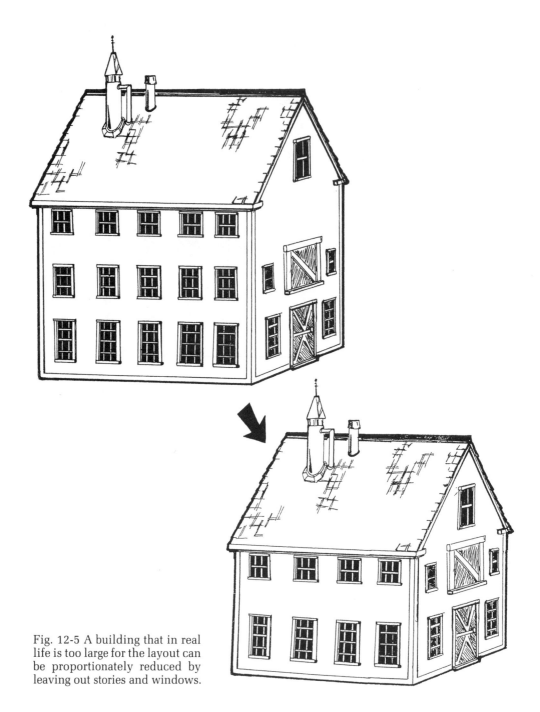

Fig. 12-5 A building that in real life is too large for the layout can be proportionately reduced by leaving out stories and windows.

Fig. 12-6 These four buildings are actually cardboard boxes with color photocopies of model building fronts glued to them! Detail parts such as awnings and ventilation shafts were added, and the result is surprisingly realistic. These buildings would work well toward the rear of an industrial layout.

the layout needs more life, but these last-minute decisions create a lot of unnecessary work. Try to include all structures on the original layout plans. Buildings on a narrow-gauge line are usually constructed near the track so that the freight and cargo can be loaded to the rolling stock with ease.

Draw the outline of the building on the layout with a grease pencil or marking pen. This will give an accurate blueprint of the building locations. You can then apply plaster or plastic scenery everywhere but directly on the building site. Leave $\frac{1}{4}$-inch or so of space around the outline to allow for the structure's foundation. The building can later be fitted to the layout with additional plaster or installed before the ground-cover texture, both of which will fill in any gaps between the building base and the layout.

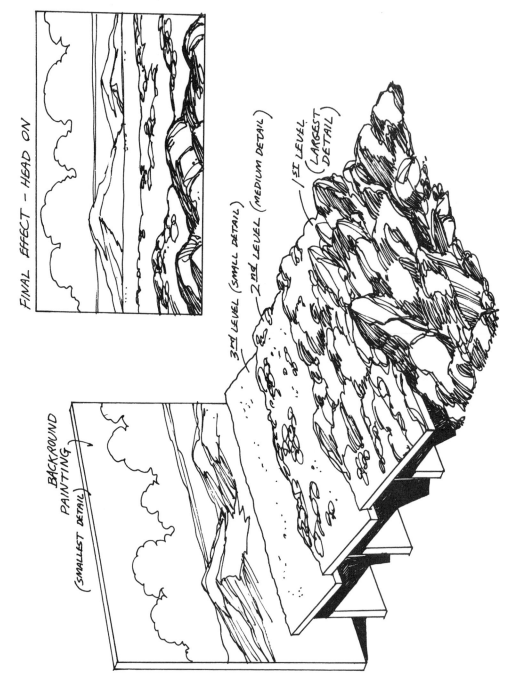

Fig. 12-7 This method of forced perspective uses unconnected levels that are tilted slightly to overlap.

190

Fig. 12-8A Forced perspective fools the eye into believing that these men are equal size.

Fig. 12-8B This view reveals the true relationships.

FORCED PERSPECTIVE

Forced perspective is an old trick used by modelers in the film industry to increase apparent distance. With this technique, small layouts and dioramas can be made to appear larger. Forced perspective uses diminishing scales, with the largest models placed directly in front of the viewer and the smallest models placed farthest from the viewer. By moving from HO scale to N scale, the perceived distance between foreground and background is at least doubled. When you make such a dramatic shift in scale, make sure that you don't place buildings of two different scales close to one another. I have found that placing the smaller-scale buildings behind and on a different plane from the foreground produces startlingly realistic results. The backdrop can also be used to enhance this illusion of depth. Painted scenery on the backdrop gives a three-dimensional look. The layout scenery and structures should be constructed and placed in relation to the backdrop with a center point of perspective. This is where the

Fig. 12-9 This highly condensed version of the often modified and frequently reincarnated AHM/Revell/ConCor engine house has great detail and has been a popular seller for more than twenty years. I cut the model in half lengthwise and eliminated one window in length. The weathering was done with an acrylic wash.

viewer's attention will automatically be drawn. Structures should be placed with rooflines directed toward this perspective point.

Once you have decided what you are going to build, you must decide how you are going to build it. Although beautifully detailed buildings can be built from scratch, there are so many excellent kits available that most modelers at least begin with them.

STRUCTURE CONVERSIONS

A major difficulty in modeling realistic structures from kits is to produce an original design. Most of the dozens of building kits on the market have already appeared in hundreds of photographs in one book or another. It makes no difference how these buildings are placed on a layout or what

Fig. 12-10 I built this engine house so that the base could be permanently mounted, but the entire structure could be removed for detailing or maintenance. Two of these tiny Movie Miniatures locomotives could fit here on the ready track.

colors they are painted. If the buildings are from the same kit, they will always look alike unless they are heavily modified. This problem is unique to structures. You expect to see thousands of almost-identical boxcars, but you don't expect to see more than one of Dale's Dingies. Ironically, most model railroaders tend to purchase as many different freight cars as possible, yet they buy the same structures that appear on other model railroads and build them just the way they come out of the box.

Most structure kits can be easily modified during assembly. The walls and roofs can be cut or altered so that when complete the building is unique. Using one or more kits to make something entirely different is called cross-kitting or kitbashing (see Chapter 8). Cross-kitting works just as well on buildings as it does on locomotives and rolling stock; in fact, it's much easier and more rewarding.

Fig. 12-11 If you're clever, you can produce a completely new structure using nothing but leftover parts, as was done here.

Imagination is the key in structure conversions, so when milling through building kits, try to think of each kit as nothing more than a box of parts or raw materials, rather than a complete building. Combining the parts of several kits into one big box and discarding the instructions will almost force you to create an original design.

You will need at least two kits to make a conversion because extra parts are often needed to redesign a building. You might want to convert a building to two stories instead of one, or use the windows and doors from one kit on another. Always save leftover kit parts for future conversions. When making major changes in a kit, you might want to add interior braces for strength. Cardboard or thin plastic can be added as interior walls to prevent a vacant, hollow-shell appearance.

I will show you step by step how to convert a typical single-structure kit into two complete buildings that can be used for any layout. The kit we will modify is the freight station originally manufactured by Revell. It has since gone through several metamorphoses and is currently being produced by Con-Cor. It retains the original style, but one end has been

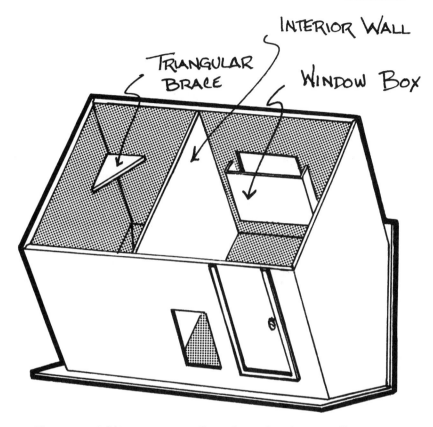

INTERIOR WALL

TRIANGULAR BRACE

WINDOW BOX

Fig. 12-12 Adding interior walls and window boxes will increase a building's realism and also strengthen it.

cut short and a smaller office attached. From this simple kit, we will extract a fire station typical of western towns around the turn of the century and a short-line way station. You may also want to purchase another kit, the Revell/AHM Schoolhouse, for the spare parts necessary for a complete conversion.

The Fire Station

The fire station in Figure 12-13 is not the type you would find in an urban area such as Los Angeles or San Francisco, unless it was in an old section of town. Most urban fire companies were located in ornate buildings that included such luxuries as gas lighting, stained-glass windows, and spotless equipment. This building is the type born of necessity with

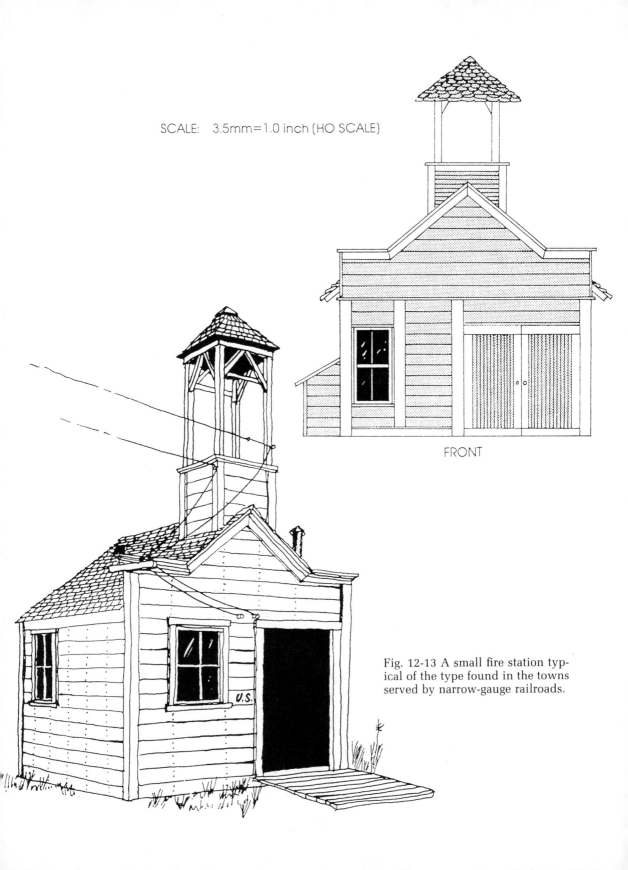

SCALE: 3.5mm=1.0 inch (HO SCALE)

FRONT

U.S.

Fig. 12-13 A small fire station typical of the type found in the towns served by narrow-gauge railroads.

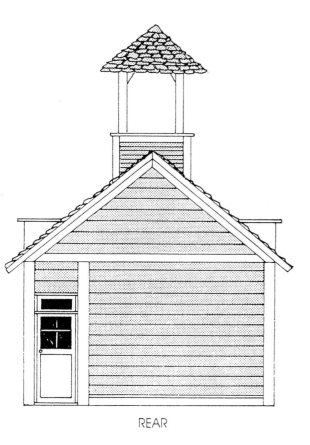

REAR

Fig. 12-14A, B, and C Front, rear, and side views of the fire station.

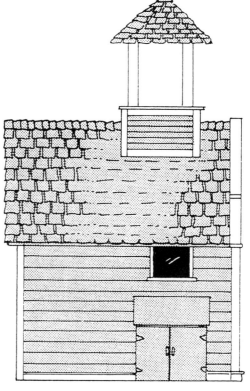

SIDE (Opposite side similar without window or storage box)

Fig. 12-15A and B Front and back views of the completed fire station.

a minimum of frills, yet it still has the class of some of the urban structures with its bright paint, brass bell, false front, and gold-leaf lettering.

Begin construction by finding the kit walls that match the sketches of the fire station. You should be able to see immediately where and how these parts must be cut. The front wall starts with the section with the shovel and freight door. Cut off the left-hand portion flush with the small window, using an X-Acto saw to ensure even, straight cuts. Cut off the right-hand portion of the wall flush with the freight-door molding. Cut one slat out of the door opening at the top. Save every piece you cut out because you will use most of these parts later.

A new door can be scratch-built using Plastruct sheet and Evergreen scribed sheet styrene. It is easy to construct and should take no longer than three minutes. Simply cut out a square of scribed styrene the shape of the door and glue on pieces of .010 strips. An alternative would be to use the stock freight door, but this wouldn't look prototypical.

The top half of the station, the false-front portion, is made up of pieces of the station base spliced together. Strips of styrene are glued in place for molding. An easier, more expensive alternative would be to use .040 inch Evergreen plastic with .125-inch-board spacing. This material is fantastic, so don't be bashful about buying a supply to augment your Plastruct shapes. The flagpole is from the schoolhouse kit, or it can be purchased separately at a model railroad shop. The bulletin board is one end of the freight station with the roof peak cut off at the first board down. File the ends flat and square to remove the beveled edge.

The back wall is the portion of the station with the ladder attached. Cut off the left portion of the wall, leaving enough room for a small, single door. Glue the trim piece from the left side onto the extreme right side of the finished wall. Check the width against the front wall as you make your cuts and additions. The peak can be made from the floorboards or constructed from Evergreen and Plastruct as described for the front wall. Be sure to match exactly the peak and pitch of the front wall.

The final side wall is made up of spliced-together pieces that were left over from the previous steps. The splice lines are hidden by plumbing lines. The coal bin is from the schoolhouse kit.

Cut the schoolhouse roof down to fit the length of the new side walls, leaving a slight overhang at the rear and sides. The front of the roof will butt against the false front. The ladder, roof vent, and bell tower are all taken from the schoolhouse kit. The ladder should be cut down and mounted as shown in Figure 12-15B. The bell tower is kit stock, but you'll need to file the base to fit the new roof angle.

After completely assembling the building, apply a light coat of primer. This will make it easier to hand-paint the detail pieces and will give the finished model a dull, lifelike appearance. The basic walls should be painted flat Tuscan Red with flat white trim. To achieve this combination, use Pactra's Hull Red mixed with a small amount of Insignia Red. The trim color is Pactra's Light Gray, which is actually white with just a drop of black to alleviate the snowy look. The roof should be painted with flat Slate Gray or Gun Metal. If you are brush-painting the structure, don't worry if brush marks show; these will disappear when you weather the structure. The lettering "Engine Co. No. 1" is something I found in my spare parts box, which was left over from an old MPC hotrod kit. You can use Letra-Set rub-on letters or any spare decals that you might have.

Fire stations such as this were usually manned by volunteers, so no one would be at the building unless there was a fire. However, I wanted to have a permanent member like the larger companies, so I have a resident fire chief made out of a Preiser conductor. The equipment would include a Jordan fire engine and a hose car made from a modified Snap-A-Roo. Other fire-fighting equipment that might be included would be hoses, shovels, ladders, and buckets.

The entire project took only three easy evenings, although it will take more time if you decide to add interior detail and the wheeled equipment. Don't forget to save the extra pieces, which will be necessary to model the way station.

The Way Station

To construct the way station, you will need the wall and floor parts that form the office from the Revell/AHM freight station kit, the extra roof from the Atlas Platform kit, and a piece of Plastruct sheet plastic.

Assemble the three walls of the freight station as described in the kit instructions, then file the top flat. Build a duplicate of the long, windowed wall using scribed Plastruct ABS sheet to finish the basic structure. Glue the Atlas roof to the top of the building, leaving a little overhang on one end. Glue the stock Atlas gable (part No. 17) to either end of the roof. These parts will hide the fact that the basic building shell is incomplete from the roof baseline up.

Cut the Revell wood floor to the same dimensions as the base of the roof and glue it to the bottom of the building, centering it under the gables.

Use the same paint mixture of Tuscan Red as described for the fire station to paint the basic shell of the way station. Paint the roof and station platform flat tan with a light wash of flat black. Paint the trim light gray and weather the entire structure. Add detail parts from the Revell Freight

Fig. 12-16 The completed way station.

Station kit, such as barrels, crates, light fixtures, and benches. Don't be bashful about details. Small structures such as this were loaded with clutter.

Interior detail can also be added using SS Ltd. parts, such as a desk, ticket booth, lamps, potbellied stove, chair, or scales. Allow your imagination free reign. Place the station on your layout close to the tracks, but be careful that the roof overhang doesn't obstruct them.

BUILDING COMPONENTS AND EXTERIORS

While there is an enormous quantity of preformed kits available, eventually the time will come when you will want or need to create a building from the foundation up. Following are some common building components and ways in which you can create them.

Foundations

When creating realistic model buildings, one of the most important details that modelers often forget is to blend the building foundation into the surrounding scenery. There should be no gaps or shadows between the foundation and the earth or pavement. Blocks of wood or cardboard scraps can be used for supports so that the structure will blend into the surrounding landscape with all walls level.

Fig. 12-17 Incorrect and correct blending of building foundations into the scenery.

Many buildings in real life are not always perfectly straight and aligned, especially older buildings. Old, decrepit buildings are commonly found on narrow-gauge railroads, so perhaps a few of the structures should lean slightly or have "crumbling" foundations. However, if your structures tilt or lean excessively, they will detract from the realism of an otherwise perfect layout. The bottom edge of the building can be shaved with a knife or sanded on one side to make the walls uneven. Outside trim and moldings can be glued with a slight bow in the center to simulate a building that has "settled" with age. Books such as the Sunset series on ghost towns contain excellent photos that show the ravages of time.

Clapboard Siding

One of the most widely used siding patterns is clapboard. While most often seen on houses, it is also used on railroad stations and other public buildings. Clapboard is composed of a series of equal-width wood strips layered on top of one another, similar to roofing shingles. It can be purchased ready-made in plastic or vacuum-formed sheets, or you can scratch-build your own using thin strips of styrene or wood glued to a thin piece of balsa.

When modeling clapboard siding, it is important to get the right angle of the wood strips. This is also important when applying roofing shingles. Otherwise, the angle will be off, which will result in the wood strips projecting out instead of down. Before applying the first clapboard, take a smaller strip of wood (half as wide as the strip being used for the siding) and glue it to the building shell as close as possible to the base. When dry, apply the first clapboard strip over the glued piece of wood, with both ends matched at the base of the structure.

Board and Batten Siding

Board and batten siding, inexpensive and easy to model, is composed of a series of boards (or plywood sheets) nailed to the building framework, with small strips of wood (bats) attached vertically. It is used on train stations, private homes, engine houses, and outhouses.

Evergreen strips in appropriate scale can be used for the bats. The "boards" are Evergreen's V-groove scribed siding. The grooves serve as a guide, helping to keep the bats equally spaced and vertically straight. Hold the bat strips with tweezers and apply liquid cement. Attach the bats to the siding grooves. They can be aligned slightly while the cement is still wet, but don't worry if they're not perfectly straight; a slight misalignment looks more realistic, as though the siding has warped.

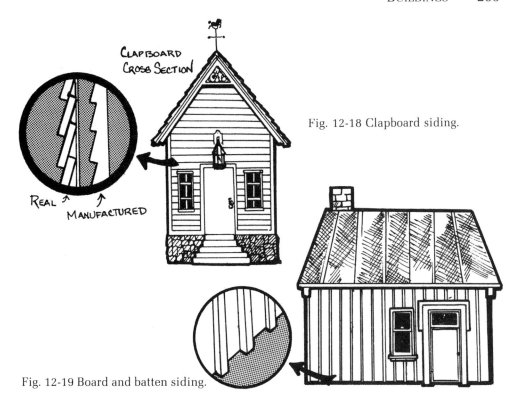

Fig. 12-18 Clapboard siding.

Fig. 12-19 Board and batten siding.

Brick and Stone

Brick and stone were widely used for structures between 1880 and 1940. These two materials provide a sturdy structure in a variety of designs. There are many ways to model brick and stone. Vacuum-formed or scribed sheets of plastic can be bought ready-made; all you have to do is cut the pieces you need. Miniature rocks and bricks can be purchased and applied individually to the building using scale mortar. Brick paper is also commercially available, and it can be applied to the building shell with adhesive.

Casting Walls

For fabricating structures such as brick buildings, where a basic design is repeated, casting is ideal for the modeler. A mold can be made of the basic pattern and then cast as many times as needed.

The first step in casting walls is to make a pattern master. If you use a latex mold, you can use almost any material to create the original pattern. Scale bricks purchased at a hobby store can be laid into a wall section, then used as a master to create as many miles of brick walls as you need.

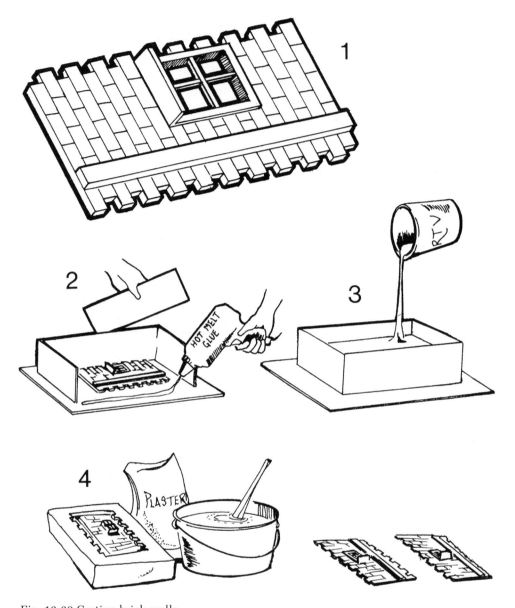

Fig. 12-20 Casting brick walls.

Do a good job on the master; every detail, as well as every error, will show. Whenever designing a pattern master, always try to include some type of flange that will interlock one casting to another. This helps to eliminate gaps between each piece.

Using the same procedures outlined for making rubber molds in Chapter 9, build a box around the master. If casting for a wood pattern, paint the master with latex paint; otherwise the wood will swell and ruin the mold. Continue with the mold-making procedure and apply five or six additional coats of latex, allowing each layer to dry thoroughly before applying the next. The final layer should be very thick, and gauze can be embedded in the latex for added strength. A fan or hair dryer can be used to speed up the curing process.

Ordinary molding plaster such as Hydrocal can be used for large pieces; small, thin patterns can be cast from a harder plaster like Castolite. Wash the mold thoroughly before each casting and spray it with a diluted detergent-and-water mixture. Mix the plaster and gently pour it into the mold; try to avoid splashing because it will create air bubbles. Give the plaster a few minutes to start setting up and then press both mold halves together. Allow them to dry completely before removing the casting.

Roofing Materials

The most common roofing materials are wood, asphalt, and tiles. Like siding, shingles can be bought in plastic sheets, cut individually from small wood pieces, or purchased as printed shingle paper. If you decide to apply individual wood shingles, see the section on clapboard siding in this chapter to achieve the correct angle for application. Real shingled roofs come in a small variety of colors, including black, green, red, white, and slate gray. Paint the shingles in uneven, vertical strokes. Try to avoid a uniform coat of color, and weather the shingles heavily.

Scribed plastic or styrene can be used to simulate corrugated metal roofs. The scribed lines should be as close together as possible, depending upon the scale you are using. For HO scale, the lines should be no farther apart than $\frac{1}{32}$ of an inch.

Corrugated metal roofs are common on coaling stations, trailer depots, engine houses, and even some rustic outhouses. Paint the finished roof with a coat of flat silver paint to simulate iron, aluminum, or tin. Weather the roof thoroughly, adding "rust" (acrylic paint color) as needed.

Sheets of asphalt roofing can be simulated with several materials. The most common is fine-grit emery paper, which can be purchased at any

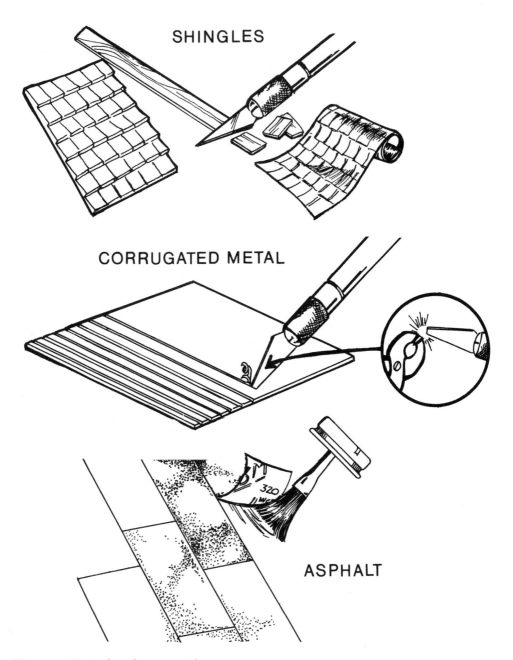

SHINGLES

CORRUGATED METAL

ASPHALT

Fig. 12-21 Typical roofing materials.

paint or hardware store and is available in black. Apply it to the roof of the structure with contact cement. Masking tape or surgical tape can also be used and then sprayed with paint.

Windows and Doors

Windows are generally the focal point of a structure and often carry with them the major components of the building's architectural design. Windows and doors can be purchased premade, but you will have to make do with the sizes available. Grandt produces a line of beautifully detailed windows and doors, as well as other architectural components. However, if you cannot find the precise window or door you want, scratchbuilding is not difficult.

To scratchbuild windows and doors, use Evergreen's styrene strips to make the door and window framework. Do not use wood, since the grain is too large and will look entirely out of scale. For true-to-life windows, extremely thin, clear plastic can be used to simulate glass. This clear plastic can be glued to the inside of the building shell, mounted to the window openings, and then the framework constructed over it.

Now that you have an idea of some of the techniques you can use to create specific architectural effects, we'll discuss how you can use these techniques to create specific buildings for your layout.

MODELING A PROTOTYPE STRUCTURE

A familiar building often found near a railroad is the outhouse. While they are unusual in the city, railroads in the country before 1940 often had more outhouses than telephone poles. If your layout is set in a time period prior to 1920, an outhouse should be included for every station, house, or factory. For narrow-gauge railroading, they are a must. Narrow-gauge lines rarely had such luxuries as indoor plumbing; in fact, they were often lucky to have outhouses!

Real railroads frequently had plans drawn up for structures that were used often. Books of standard designs were published for everything from track ties and trestles to stations and outhouses. Outhouse designs are all basically the same, differing only in the location of their doors and the number of stalls.

Model outhouses are easy to make and can be a good first scratchbuilt model. They can be made just a bit different simply by using board and batten or a novelty siding, as well as different color schemes. Barn-red outhouses, for example, are intended for use by railroad employees and

1. GLUE CLEAR PLASTIC BEHIND WINDOW
2. LOWER WINDOW FRAME   OPENING
3. UPPER WINDOW FRAME
4. SASH AND SILL
5. DOOR FRAME
6. DOOR AND MOLDING

Fig. 12-22 Door and window construction.

located near the engine houses or section houses. Green and white outhouses would be for the general public and located near the railroad stations or behind private homes. A wide variety of ventilation devices were used, from a series of round, bored holes to rectangular slats cut in the siding. The stacks themselves were often made from wood planks nailed

SCALE: 3.5 MM = 1 FOOT

Fig. 12-23B Plans for a one-seat outhouse.

Fig. 12-23A The lowly outhouse is the most common—and most often ignored—of all structures found along narrow-gauge railways.

into a square tube with a vent on the side and a cap of some type to keep rainwater out.

To model an outhouse, you must draw up plans and pattern pieces. The standard size for a two-stall outhouse is 5 × 8 feet. The stall doors measure approximately 24 inches across. When using novelty siding, make sure the grooves all run horizontally on the pattern pieces. Board and batten should run vertically. Two-stall outhouses with doors that butt together must have an interior floor to brace the sides and ends. Two-stall outhouses with doors centered must have an interior roof, as well as an interior floor, to brace the door-divider piece.

One-stall outhouses often have centered doors, so only an interior floor will be necessary for support. The roof can be modified from a leftover roof kit or made from scratch using plastic wood shingle sheets. Evergreen makes scale 6 × 6-inch strips that are perfect for the vent stacks. Cut angles to match the rooflines and opposite angles for the rain cap to rest on. On single-stall outhouses, the vent stacks are mounted to one corner. Two-stall outhouses have their vent stacks centered between the two stalls.

If you paint the outhouse only one color, assemble it completely (with the exception of the roof) before painting. For contrasting trim, assemble and paint the main shell one color. Paint corner trim and door frames another color, then attach to the main body.

There are many other types of structures that can be included on your layout. It all depends upon the purpose of the narrow-gauge train and the time period you are re-creating. Research your train's prototype and make notes of its surrounding structures. At this point, it is your decision what to include, and whether you will buy premade buildings, model one from a kit, or scratchbuild an original.

Super-Detailing

Painting is the final step in a long chain of difficult modeling operations. If you make a mistake at this stage, you can ruin an otherwise perfect model. I've seen many models ruined by slipshod work such as a grainy finish, color runs, and inappropriate color choices. On the other hand, I've seen some models that were masterpieces, yet they were nothing more than carefully finished stock kits. A good paint job can make even the lowly snap-kit look as though it had been made by a pro. If you follow the steps in order in this chapter and don't try to be creative at first, you should get acceptable and pleasing results.

PREPARING THE MODEL

Many modelers believe that the biggest paint problem is in the application, but the secret of a beautiful paint finish is in the preparation. The two most important steps in the preparation are cleaning and priming. When handling a model, the oil from your skin can cause the paint to dimple and flake off unless the surface of the model has been prepared properly. Primer cuts through most dirts and oils and gives the surface a texture for the paint to adhere to. The best type of primer is the automotive lacquer-gray spray type. This primer can be used on either plastic or metal with equally good results. On plastic, apply a light dust coat before applying a thicker prime coat; this will prevent the lacquer from attacking and crazing the plastic surface.

Any bad spots on the model, such as pits or cracks, should be filled with putty and wet-sanded smooth. One good putty is Ditzler DFL-1 gray

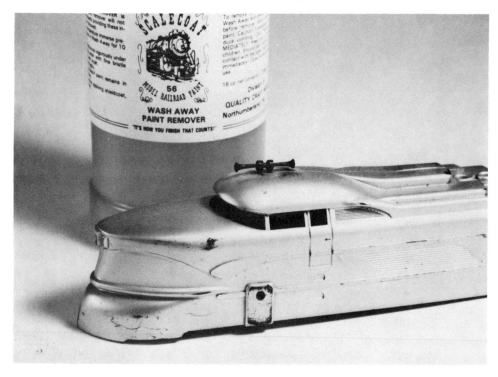

Fig. 13-1 Model railroaders no longer have to live with poor paint or paint over a model's original surface. Now, thanks to Scalecoat, most plastic kits such as this rare old Mantua diesel can be stripped without damage.

spot putty, which is available at automotive supply stores. This is not as grainy as the commercially available green hobby putty, and when applied in thin coats it can be sanded in half an hour. Thicker coats will take longer to dry. Having a perfectly smooth model will enable you to effect a smooth paint job.

When all putty work on the model is complete, sand the entire model with 400-grit wet-and-dry sandpaper. Lightly wash the model and thoroughly dry it with a lint-free cloth or hair dryer. Apply a coat of primer to the model to show up any bad spots that you missed during the preliminary sanding. If the primer coat discloses a spot that requires more work, sand through the primer before reapplying more putty. Clean the model, prime, and recheck for bad spots. Apply a final coat of primer and allow it to dry for about 8 hours. Try not to apply too many coats of primer or too thick a coat or the primer will obscure details. When dry, wet-sand

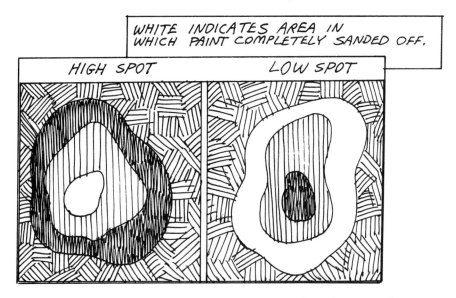

Fig. 13-2 If the model is rough, alternate different colors of primer. This way you will see which low and high spots still need work.

the model lightly with 600-grit wet-and-dry sandpaper. Be careful not to sand through the primer coats.

The last step before painting is to mask off areas that either will be painted another color or will be left unpainted. For the best masking job, use drafting tape rather than standard masking tape. Masking tape applied over paint may pull off the paint as the tape is removed; drafting tape won't. Clear Scotch Magic tape is the most useful tape when masking two-tone paint, stripes, or lettering. It is the thinnest tape available, so it leaves only the slightest ridge at the color-separation line. This tape also has the advantage of remaining cloudy where it has not adhered firmly to the model's surface. The purpose of masking is to protect areas that are not to be painted. With the clear tape, you can be certain these areas are securely masked and that paint will not seep through.

AIRBRUSHING

There really is no substitute for an airbrushed paint job. An airbrush acts like a miniature scaled-down version of a real spray gun. The paint atomizes, and you can control the flow of paint to produce a fine mist spray. You also have the ability to control the width of the spray. A good painter can produce a fine line or blend from one color to another. Both of these techniques are impossible with a brush.

At first, you may feel that a spray can gives satisfactory results and that the added expense of an airbrush is unnecessary. This is fine for the amateur modeler, but if you want to be professional and achieve the best finish possible, by all means get an airbrush and compressor. The expense will be worthwhile down the line and should be considered an investment. Good-quality equipment will last a lifetime if taken care of properly.

Airbrushes are marketed by a number of companies and can be purchased at nearly all hobby shops or art supply stores. There are two major types of airbrushes—single-action, external or internal mix, and dual-action. Single-action means that the control button serves only one function: It turns the air flow off and on. The paint flow is adjusted with a separate control. External mix means that the paint is mixed with air outside of

Fig. 13-3 A large compressor is expensive, but for top-quality work it is almost a necessity.

the airbrush, right at the end of the control tip. Internal mix combines paint and air inside the airbrush. Dual-action control lets you vary both the volume and pattern of spray while painting with one finger; both hands are needed to adjust a single-action brush. Select the type of airbrush that will best suit your needs. The better-quality brands are Paasche, Binks, and Thayer-Chandler. Service is an important consideration when purchasing an airbrush. Choose a brand that you can get parts and supplies for easily and you will save yourself much frustration.

Another consideration when selecting an airbrush is the type of paint containers available. Open-top color cups are handy for small jobs, but for most modeling purposes the siphon bottle is preferred for its greater capacity, and it has less chance of spilling. Binks makes an airbrush whose siphons have caps that fit Floquil bottles, so paint can be sprayed directly from the storage container.

An airbrush requires a good, steady supply of air. Aerosol cans (Propel) of refrigerant gas are available for airbrushes, but they last only for 10 or 15 minutes. If you intend to do a lot of airbrushing, buying can after can gets expensive and tiresome. There are also several small compressors on the market designed specifically for hobby use for less than $100, but they don't have any means of regulation and are set to deliver air pressure of 25 to 30 psi. You can regulate the air pressure somewhat by loosening the connecting nut between hose and compressor. Your best bet is a large compressor with a storage tank and adjustable pressure release. While cumbersome for the average modeler, it is a good investment and can be used for other household jobs, which can justify the additional expense. A third alternative is an oxygen tank with a gauge. This is about the same price as a small compressor. The tank will give you an hour or two of continuous spraying time and can be refilled for a small fee. And it's quiet!

Preparing the Paint

The paint you use must be fresh, clean, and free of lumps. Any foreign matter in the paint will clog the airbrush. Always strain the paint through an old pair of nylon stockings or cheesecloth before running it through the airbrush. Paint for airbrushing should also be thinned more than for brush painting. Airbrushes are designed for spraying artist's tints and inks, which make most model paints look very thick. Airbrushing by the nozzle of the airbrush tends to dry out the mixture, making the paint thicker and drier by the time it reaches the surface of the model.

The proper thinning ratio for most paints is 30 to 50 percent thinner

Fig. 13-4 A good paint strainer can be made from a nylon stocking cemented or glued to a piece of twisted wire.

to paint. This amount of course depends upon atmospheric conditions, the type of paint, and the type of airbrush. Experiment with thinning ratios prior to painting the model. Too much thinner will affect the stickiness and flow of the paint.

Weather is one of the most important factors to consider before starting to paint. Never try to paint when it is raining or extremely damp, since the water vapor in the air will affect the paint, causing it to blush. Conversely, extremely hot weather will cause lacquer to fog or cloud and dry too quickly, resulting in a dull finish. The best paint jobs are achieved when the temperature is between 65 and 78 degrees F.

Dust and runs are two of the biggest enemies in model painting. Runs can be eliminated for the most part by using lacquer paints and spraying carefully. Dust is a problem for even the best of painters. If you plan to build many models, it would be worthwhile to set up a spray booth. Select a well-ventilated area, preferably with some type of fan to draw excess paint fumes out through a filter. The filter and vents will trap floating particles of paint that might otherwise be inhaled. Paint fumes are toxic and constitute a fire hazard. To construct a portable bench-top spray booth, see my earlier book, *Model Building Handbook* (also published by Chilton) for full details.

The model must be clean, dry, and dust-free for a good-quality paint job. Metal and plastic models should be washed in warm water with household detergent, rinsed thoroughly, and allowed to dry completely. Do not wash wooden models; instead, blow off sawdust and other loose material with an airbrush or the air attachment on a large compressor.

Plastic models may need protection from paint solvents. Paints such as Accu-Paint, Polly S, and Scalecoat II are safe for use directly on plastics, but Floquil and Scalecoat can attack styrene plastics. Just to be safe, first apply a protective coating such as Floquil Barrier or Scalecoat Shieldcoat so that you won't risk ruining a model you've just kitbashed or detailed extensively. Thin the protective coating about 50 percent for spraying.

You'll also need a method of holding the model while painting. Several companies, such as GB Engineering, offer handles and holders that allow you to hold and turn a model for spraying while keeping your fingers away from the wet paint. It's not necessary to go out and buy holders when you can easily devise your own using objects from around the house. A long piece of wood can be wedged with masking tape to the inside of a loco-

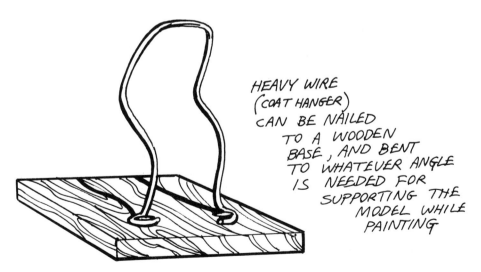

HEAVY WIRE
(COAT HANGER)
CAN BE NAILED
TO A WOODEN
BASE, AND BENT
TO WHATEVER ANGLE
IS NEEDED FOR
SUPPORTING THE
MODEL WHILE
PAINTING

Fig. 13-5 Most models need some sort of support for painting.

motive, or you can bend a wire coat hanger for a handle. If all else fails, vinyl or rubber gloves will allow you to hold the model in your hand while painting and not get your fingers dirty.

Airbrushing Techniques

The single-action airbrush should be held in one hand with the index finger over the actuator button. The other hand can be used to control paint flow at the adjusting knob. This type of unit is a little simpler to use, but it does not have the fine control of the dual-action units. The dual-action unit should be held in the same way, but remember that by pulling back on the trigger, you can also control paint flow. This is extremely handy if you want to vary line width or blend colors. You can also use the pull-back feature to clear the unit if it temporarily clogs.

When everything is ready, turn on the compressor and press the actuator button on the airbrush. While the air passes through the airbrush, set the regulator for the air pressure you want. Insert the color bottle or siphon in the control tip and test-spray on a cardboard box. This procedure will enable you to see that all equipment is working properly so that you can make any necessary adjustments before spraying the model. If you have never used an airbrush before, experiment with it until you become familiar with the painting techniques before spraying the actual model.

The techniques used for airbrushing are basically the same as those for spraying from a can. Hold the airbrush approximately 3 to 6 inches from the surface of the model, push the button, and start spraying to one side of the model. Hold your wrist steady and move the airbrush with

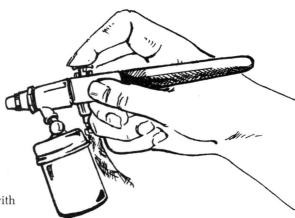

Fig. 13-6 To maintain good control with an airbrush, hold it like a pen.

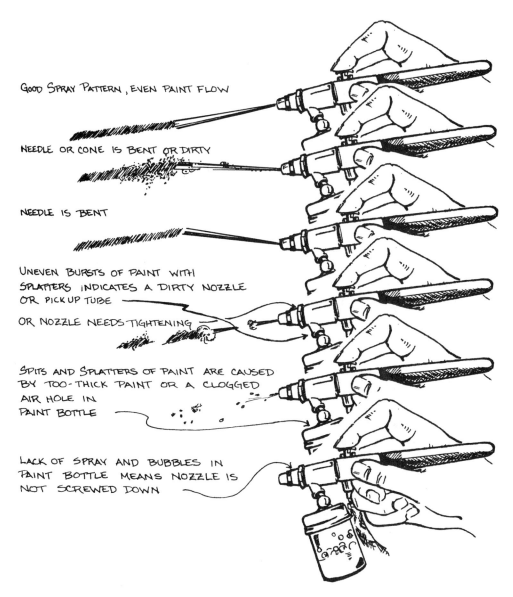

GOOD SPRAY PATTERN, EVEN PAINT FLOW

NEEDLE OR CONE IS BENT OR DIRTY

NEEDLE IS BENT

UNEVEN BURSTS OF PAINT WITH
SPLATTERS INDICATES A DIRTY NOZZLE
OR PICK UP TUBE

OR NOZZLE NEEDS TIGHTENING

SPITS AND SPLATTERS OF PAINT ARE CAUSED
BY TOO-THICK PAINT OR A CLOGGED
AIR HOLE IN
PAINT BOTTLE

LACK OF SPRAY AND BUBBLES IN
PAINT BOTTLE MEANS NOZZLE IS
NOT SCREWED DOWN

Fig. 13-7 Diagnosing a problem with an airbrush is easy if you know what to look for. Each problem has a unique set of symptoms.

your arm, sweeping past the model at an even pace. Stop spraying when the airbrush has completely passed over the model. Following this procedure will help avoid spatters and produce an even coat of paint. As you paint, watch the spray pattern closely as it sweeps over the model. The paint should go on wet and shiny, but it should look almost dry soon after it is applied. If the paint does not go on wet and dries before hitting the model, you'll get a rough, sandy texture. Paint that is too wet will not dry quickly, and possibly it will cause runs and buildups that can ruin the paint job and hide fine detail.

You will find that a single application of paint won't give an even coat of color, so continue turning and spraying the model until you have applied a single coat all over. Then go back and apply another coat. Several light coats of paint are less likely to hide details than one heavy one. Once you've mastered these basic techniques for making even, steady strokes, you will be ready to do some real painting.

Clean the airbrush immediately after use by running thinner through it. Remove the needle and wipe it off. By drawing the needle out through the front of the gun, you can avoid contaminating the rear chamber with paint. Clean out the jar or cup and wipe it out thoroughly. Chips of dry paint can ruin future paint jobs. You may have to take the entire unit apart occasionally for a thorough cleaning. Refer to the manufacturer's instructions. Occasionally, I leave all the nonplastic parts of my airbrush overnight in a sealed glass jar half full of thinner. This loosens any caked-on paint and, followed by a thorough cleaning, will keep your airbrush like new.

STRIPING, LETTERING, AND DECALING

The "make it or break it" time in model building is when it comes time to paint and detail. If you're like the average model builder, this is where you usually get stage fright. But rest assured that detailing is probably the second greatest source of satisfaction you will get from model railroading. You can create excellent models if you just follow a few simple rules and use the right equipment for the job.

The type of paint you choose for airbrushing is important. Two popular brands of paints for model railroads are Scalecoat and Floquil. Both have special formulas that provide an ultra-thin coat of paint that won't obscure the finest of details. Floquil offers a line of regular lacquer-based paints, as well as water-based paints marketed under the Polly S label, with similar colors in both lines. All of these paints are authentic colors matched to color chips from prototype railroads.

Fig. 13-8 The numbering and lettering on these railroad cars helps to give them the feel of the prototypes.

Here we will concentrate on detailing by hand, starting with brush painting and going through to the finishing touches, striping, hand lettering, and applying decals.

Brush Painting

Painting detail on models with a regular brush requires no elaborate equipment or time-consuming masking. First, select the right type of paint for brush painting. Not all paints are suitable for plastic models, and not all paints are suitable for brush painting. The best brush paints are Pactra "Namel" or Humbrol brand. Testor's normal paints are not suitable because they dry too fast.

Purchase the colors that you need and try to avoid shaking the bottles. Instead, unscrew the top and pour out and discard the oil that has accumulated on the top of the paint. Stir the remaining paint in the jar thoroughly. If you do not follow this procedure, the first coat of paint will be too transparent and another coat will be needed. Not only does a second coat of paint hide fine detail, but there is an increased chance of error. A good brush job should be achieved with only one coat of paint. A paintbrush is a tool, and if properly handled, even a cheap brush will give satisfactory results. But there is never any substitute for a good-quality brush. For large surfaces, a brush of medium width is enough. A very wide brush is most often a handicap. For small parts, choose small brushes. For a striping job, use the smallest brush available.

Adding Stripes

Stripes are probably the easiest realistic detailing to apply. They can be painted on or put on with an adhesive. Either way is simple and effective. The kind of detailing required will usually dictate the method you use. If the model is an injection-molded plastic piece, such as a Monogram or Revell, mask the area you want to stripe using regular automotive masking tape, and flow a thin coat of paint on with a size 1 brush. Lift off the tape in one smooth motion before the paint gets too tacky.

If you apply too thick a layer of paint, you will find that edges will build up along both sides of the stripe. These are difficult to smooth out, so try to avoid a thick application. When the paint is thoroughly dry, use rubbing compound to completely smooth out the paint. See the section on rubbing compound later in this chapter for full instructions.

An easier way to apply stripes to a model is to use stripes from a decal

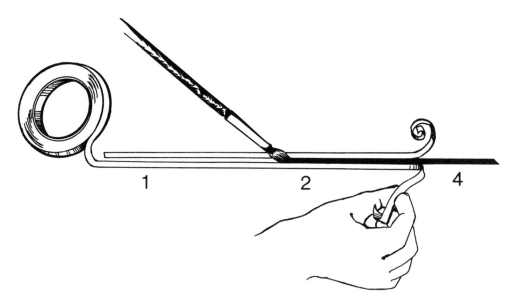

Fig. 13-9 Masking is an easy, quick, and accurate way to paint stripes, but be sure not to use too much paint.

sheet. Lay a ruler along the stripe and cut it from the decal sheet with an X-Acto knife. Make sure you stay close to the actual decal so that you get as little as possible of the "lip" or edge that surrounds every decal. Wet the stripe until it slides from its backing and slide it onto the model. Pat dry with an absorbent piece of cloth or cotton. Once it begins to dry, don't attempt to move it. At this point it is usually too late. You will only succeed in tearing it.

A decal stripe is fine on the outside of a plastic body because it is thin and will not project too far above the surface. This is not the case, however, with striping tape. While popular, this tape tends to stick out like a sore thumb when applied to the exterior of a model. If you use it, shop around until you find the thinnest tape you can get. It comes with an adhesive backing and is easily applied.

There is still another way to put stripes on your model. Many art stores carry sheets of thin acetate with lines printed on it. The printed material is as thin as paint and can be easily transferred by rubbing. The sheets come in many different trade names; one of them is Letraset. If this particular brand is not available, explain to your dealer what you need and he'll probably be able to recommend another brand. All you have to do is cut the stripe from the sheet and press it in place. Presto, instant stripes!

Lettering

A first-class job of hand lettering will set your model apart from the crowd when done correctly. Decals are fine, but when you can't find the right decal for the job, paint them or try transfer lettering, the easiest method.

Good-quality brushes are a must for hand lettering. Four different sizes will cover most situations nicely. You will need brush sizes 1, 0, 00, and 000. Size 1 is the largest, on down to the smallest, 000, which has a needle point for extremely fine work. The best brushes come from West Germany and fortunately are available at most hobby shops. Never buy a cheap brush. A good-quality brush will last for years, making the higher original cost a better value in the long run. There's nothing more discouraging than a paint brush that starts to lose its bristles in the middle of a job.

A free-flowing enamel, such as Testor's PLA enamels, is good for hand lettering. Never dip a brush into a bottle. You'll probably dip it in too far because you can't see what you're doing. This can ruin the fine tip of a brush. Before starting to paint, tip the bottle upside down, then set it upright and remove the lid. The amount of paint left in the lid is usually sufficient for hand lettering. If it needs to be thinned, add just a drop or two of Testor's thinner in the cap and mix evenly.

Pass the brush through the paint with the handle angled sharply. Roll the brush in your hand so that the point comes out looking "wet" and with a sharp point. Always make sure the paint flows smoothly from your brush. When it stops flowing, discontinue painting and dip the brush again. Avoid a buildup of paint, which is caused from too much paint flowing from the brush. Practice will really pay off.

It's a good idea to pencil the lettering lightly before beginning to paint. Guidelines will be very helpful for crisp, sharp lettering. Always clean the brush thoroughly after using it to keep the bristles fresh and pliable for a long life.

Applying Decals

Decals are designed to add details on models easily without the work and trouble involved in hand painting them. Nearly every manufacturer's trademark, as well as a variety of numbers, fields, and stripes, is available

Fig. 13-10 Don't dip a brush directly into a bottle of paint. Instead, pour a small amount into the cap and twist the brush in it.

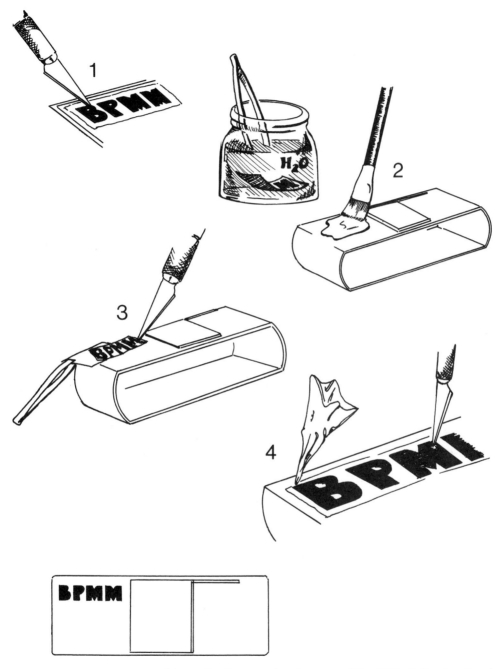

Fig. 13-11 (1) Trim the decal from the sheet as closely as possible. (2) Soak the decal and spread softening solution onto the decal area. (3) Apply the decal. (4) Blot the excess fluid and, when dry, puncture any air bubbles and reapply softener.

225

in decal form. Unfortunately, on many models they look like shiny plastic with letters on them. But with the techniques described in this section, even an amateur can make the decals look as though they were painted directly on the model.

The model surface should be prepared before applying decals, just as it should be before painting. Decals, like paint, need a clean, smooth surface to adhere to. Do not touch any surfaces to be covered with decals; your fingers leave a trace of oil that may prevent the decal from adhering properly. One solution is to apply a light coat of high-gloss clear paint on the areas to be decaled. This gloss coat should be applied with a paintbrush, or preferably with an airbrush. It's difficult to attain a thin enough layer of glossy clear paint with an aerosol can.

A decal merely consists of a few layers of colored paint (the letters and numbers) and clear paint (the backing). The paint backing has a certain amount of flexibility, which allows it to curve around the contours of a model, but this flexibility is rather stiff compared to the overall flexibility of wet paint. The decal can be softened up with decal-softening compound to allow it to fit the smallest details and tightest contours. These compounds can be purchased at any good model-railroad shop.

The next step is to trim the decals from the decal sheet. Some brands of decals, such as Micro-Scale, have individual decals on a single sheet, with the clear film ending at the end of each group of letters, but most have a solid sheet of clear film over the entire set of decals. If you use Micro-Scale decals, hold the decal sheet up to a light to see exactly where the clear film ends on each decal so you will know where to cut. For the solid decal sheets, trim as close to the edges of the letters or numbers as possible. Handle decals with tweezers until the model is complete, since oil from your fingers can affect the adhesive power of the decal.

Soak the decal in warm water. It should start to separate from the backing material in about 30 seconds. Brush the thinnest possible layer of decal softener over the area where the decal will be applied. Using a hobby knife to hold the decal itself, remove the backing material with tweezers, and apply the decal softener. Gently sponge off any excess decal softener with a tissue, dabbing near the edges of the decal. Use the tip of a hobby knife or the end of a paintbrush to move the decal where you want it. Do not press down on the decal to make it adhere to the model. The decal softener will take care of that.

When all decals have been applied and have had time to set for about half an hour, inspect each one for air bubbles. Prick each bubble with a

Fig. 13-12 An average piece of rolling stock can be made unique by careful attention to details.

sharp needle, and apply at least two final coats of decal softener over the surface of each decal using a sable brush. Allow to dry completely for about twelve hours. Inspect once again for air bubbles or any areas where the decal has not contoured snuggly to the model. If necessary, apply two more coats of decal softener and allow it to dry once again for twelve hours. When completely dry, gently rinse the surface of the model with water to remove any decal or softener residue and allow it to air dry completely. A hair dryer can also be used at a low temperature to speed up the drying process.

The final step is to spray the entire model with a light coat of clear, flat finish enamel, such as Testor's Chip Guard or Floquil Clear Coat.

FINISHING THE MODEL

Clear Coating

A clear coat applied over the final paint and decals can hide the unsightly shine of a model, hide the edges of decals, and make brush-painted finishes look as though they had been spray-painted by a profes-

Fig. 13-13 The difference between good, better, and terrific models is the amount of attention paid to details.

sional. A clear coat of high-gloss enamel can also be used to create realistic models.

On many models, you may want to retain the color of the plastic, but leaving it stock won't look very realistic; it will have that "plastic toy" look. Flat clear paint sprayed over the plastic will dull the shine and texture it. Model structure kits can also benefit from a coat of clear flat paint, making them appear more lifelike, as if weathered by sun and rain. Clear spray paint is also an excellent protection for the model's finish. Both the paint and decals will stand up to more handling if they are protected.

Dullcote and Glosscote are both brands names for dull or gloss clear lacquer-based paints. They can be safely applied to almost any paint or plastic, but test them on a sample scrap before applying directly on a model. As with most spray paints, the finish will turn out better if both the model and paint are at normal room temperature. A dust-free environment is also a plus.

TERRIFIC!

Clear gloss paint produces the highest gloss and the smoothest finish when sprayed 10 to 12 inches from the model in smooth, even strokes, starting the spray just off to the edge of the model and passing over the model completely before letting up on the spray. It is more difficult to tell how much paint has been applied because there will be no color change, so to prevent runs or sags spray on two or more thin coats of clear paint.

Dull clear paint will produce the least gloss and the flattest finish if held about 18 to 24 inches from the model. Use the same spraying technique as described for clear gloss paint. Several coats of Dullcote work best, with each coat quickly "dusted" over the model. Allow each coat to dry completely before applying the next.

Removing Paint from Plastic

The only equipment you will need to remove paint from plastic is a toothbrush and Cox Thimble-Drome Glow Fuel, K & B fuel, or a commercial model-paint remover. These fuels will not craze the plastic, but they will remove most paint. Dip the toothbrush into the fuel and brush over the plastic briskly. Let it set for a few minutes to allow the paint to soften. For best results, rub in the direction of the scribe and contour lines. After all paint has been removed, scrub the model with warm soapy water to remove all residue. Rinse thoroughly.

Polishing with Rubbing Compound

Rubbing compound brings out the luster in lacquer and plastic when the surfaces are polished. Since most models are small, you can't be sloppy in your technique, either in painting or polishing. You'll need rubbing compound and a soft rag such as an old T-shirt. To hold a polishing cloth correctly, push your index finger into the middle of the cloth and then flip it over your finger. Twist the top of the rag so that it pulls tight around your fingertip. Tuck the twist and excess back into your hand.

Apply the compound to an area about two inches square. Rub back and forth with firm but not hard strokes. Occasionally wet the tip of the cloth in a small cup of water. Color on the rag shows that the compound is cutting. The first few strokes are made with more pressure than the final polishing ones. As the polished shine starts to come out, let up on the pressure and start buffing lightly. Find a clean area on the rag and repeat the process, but do not use the compound this time. Wet the rag only slightly and buff the paint until you get a brilliant gloss. Use rubbing compound instead of, or after, the gloss coat.

WEATHERING

Careful attention to small details can add immeasurably to the appearance and realism of a train model and set it apart from the crowd. The technique can be as simple as adding a thin wash to the smokestack of a steam locomotive or as complex as a collapsed wooden trestle bridge. It's these small touches that apparently go unnoticed that add to the greatest sense of reality. I always add little details to our movie models that I know will not register in the mind of an observer, but will add to the illusion.

Streaking and Highlighting

Suppose you are re-creating a train line running through steep mountainous scenery. The average modeler will paint the train some standard color, create mountains from plaster, and add a few trees and rocks. The better modeler will airbrush streaks on the train, paint shadows and high-lights on the rocks and mountains, and include a variety of trees and bushes. The super-detailer will take the time to research narrow-gauge trains with lines through mountainous regions. The details would include sharp projecting rocks with stratification lines, dead trees, a small mountain stream zigzagging between rocks, and perhaps a rabbit darting through the underbrush. The possibilities are endless, but you get the idea. Take the time to think about the scene you are creating and many clever details will come to mind.

As a different approach to modeling, weathering can produce inter-esting, realistic pieces, but it requires the right technique. Too much "weathering" or the wrong technique can ruin the effect. The first step in weathering a model is to observe the actual object. Look for such things as worn paint and small dents. Notice the way dust collects under the eaves and around the trucks, and how the color of rust can vary from a dull brown to orange. Note anything else that contributes to that "used" look. If possible, watch real trains in action and take plenty of pictures to

Fig. 13-14 One of the artists at the shop is weathering a building used in a recent commercial. We use black washes so much that we try to keep a premixed batch on hand at all times.

help you remember details. You'll discover that very few of the cars are ever the same color, even those that belong to the same prototype railroad and are supposed to be the same shade. These subtle coloring differences are not the results of poor paint, but rather the effects of nature.

Unlike other railroads, most narrow-gauge trains rarely have fresh-from-the-shop paint jobs. Narrow-gauge cars will show varying degrees of exposure to the elements. The sun bleaches the paint, dust and mud kicked up from the roadbed discolors the paint, and rain washes and settles the dust into rivets and seams, causing rust to form. There will be spots where the paint has peeled, and rust will form here also. The cars will also show traces of the cargo they carry; streaks of beige grain dust or light gray concrete, or black streaks from fuel-oil spillage. Cars serving coal-mining areas will develop a blackish hue, while those that travel through desert areas will be sun bleached and sandblasted.

There are basically two methods to produce weathered effects on a model, and both work equally well. The most familiar method is to paint the weathering on, using washes of thinned-down paint. Or you can achieve basically the same results using powdered artist's chalks.

Chalking

Before applying chalk to weather a model, you should first spray the model with a light spray of clear flat paint such as Dullcote to protect the decals and paint. Even unpainted models should receive this protective coating of paint. Allow the clear finish to dry overnight.

There are dozens of brands of suitable chalks on the market that can be used to weather models. The brand with the largest variety of colors is Nupastel. It is available in individual sticks and can be purchased at most art supply stores. To begin with, you will need only a simple assortment of grays and browns. These colors can be mixed to provide just about any shade necessary for basic weathering. You will also need at least three different sizes of paintbrushes; sizes 000 and 1 and a brush with a $\frac{1}{2}$ inch tip will be sufficient to begin with.

The first step is to grind the chalk into powder. One way to do this is to rub the chalk stick on a piece of sandpaper. Never rub the chalks directly on the model; the colors will be too dark and look artificial. The chalk powder can be dry-brushed as is or mixed with just a touch of water for a different effect. Practice both techniques on a scrap piece of cardboard before applying chalk to the model to get the feel of it and to determine color intensities.

Fig. 13-15 The shingles, siding, and chimney were shaded for emphasis.

With careful strokes and just a touch of powder, you can softly shade the entire side of a boxcar to give it that subtle look of sun bleaching. Thicker mixtures of water and powder can be used for rust and grease stains. The trucks and lower edges of all rolling stock should receive the most weathering and show the most sign of rust. You'll find that with practice you can control the intensity of wet chalk powder well enough to produce rust streaks or oil dribbles, and perhaps even create weathered boards on a wooden boxcar. Apply a coat of clear flat paint to seal the chalk after each application. Allow it to dry completely before applying more chalk, then seal with paint. The clear paint will sometimes fade the chalks and soften their effect, so you may have to repeat this process several times to attain the effect you desire.

Painted Weathering

Weathering with paint is more difficult than with chalk because you run the risk of dissolving the model's paint and lettering or decals. It takes only a few brush strokes before the paint will soften and begin to blend with the weathering. Unless you are trying to achieve an extremely weathered effect—where the paint and lettering has begun to oxidize and run down the side of the car—you can ruin the model.

The airbrush is one of the best tools for applying weathering to a model. By the time the paint is sprayed on the model, it is almost dry, so there is less worry of dissolving the paint and lettering job you worked so hard on. The best way to apply weathering is in several light coats of subtle shading; this is the area where an airbrush excels. Any good-quality airbrush can be adjusted to apply a barely perceptible coat of paint. The air-compressor regulator should be adjusted for an air pressure up to 32 psi. The paint should be thinned, with nine parts thinner to one part paint, for the slightest hint of color.

If you are just learning to weather, consider using water-based paints such as the Polly S brand. This type of paint is easy to control and will not eat away at the base paint. And if you don't like the results, the paint can be washed off with water. When you are satisfied with the weathering, apply a finishing coat of clear flat paint for protection.

A mixture of one part Floquil RR-13 Grimy Black, two parts Burnt Umber F-72, and seven parts clear will produce a blackish-gray soot color that can be used for a variety of weathering effects. Floquil's Grimy Black can also be used straight from the bottle to create oil dribbles for tank cars that transport fuel. Rust can be created using Floquil's orange-colored Rust mixed with varied amounts of Roof Brown. All weathering of course will depend upon the function, location, and environment of your model railroad.

CREATING CLUTTER

Basic clutter surrounding your scenery is the super-detail that will provide that final touch of realism. You can spend hours creating towering mountains with rock cliffs, hand lettering and weathering the train, and casting resin streams so real you can almost see the water moving, but the layout will still look like a model until you add clutter. Dead trees, fallen limbs and leaves, scattered rocks and weeds are all necessary debris to add a lifelike touch. Clutter is important when modeling narrow-gauge trains, for they usually serve rural and industrial areas where civilization is most primitive.

There is an incredible selection of commercial products available to duplicate debris. Thumb through the pages of a railroad catalog and you will see hundreds of scale metal castings for barrels, industrial wheels, pipes and pipe fittings, gears, and hand tools. There are even miniature chains, hooks, and cable, railroad spikes, rail joiners, and tiny nuts and bolts. For true ease in creating clutter, Chooch produces slabs of precolored and weathered epoxy moldings of junk and scrap. These can be cut to size with a jeweler's saw and fitted anywhere on a layout or diorama.

Modeling your own clutter, however, is the easiest part of super-detailing. Most debris can be created from materials lying around the house or shop. Fine twig ends from hedges or weeds make realistic fallen limbs and branches for forest scenery. Sewing thread can be used for rope, and carefully painted facial tissue will resemble tarps or cloth sacks. Meat skewers cut into small pieces can represent cans or short pieces of pipe. The only limit is your imagination.

FIGURES

Narrow-gauge trains are small, and using a person as a scale reference helps to convey their size quickly and easily. It simultaneously adds life, drama, and activity to the model while giving a scale size that we all recognize. Painting, modifying, or creating figures can be a fascinating, frustrating education—and a thoroughly engrossing part of this hobby. The procedures and skills required are not all that difficult, and they can add much to the finished model.

Painting and detailing techniques are not that different from other types of modeling. Read this section carefully because the techniques described are as valuable to the modeler as they are to the figure painter. Painted figures often suffer from the same flat appearance that an un-weathered building does. Remember that nature abhors solid, shiny colors and squeaky-clean items and you'll never go wrong. Anything that hasn't just been built will show signs of wear, deterioration, and weathering. If you paint a conductor with glossy baby blue paint and wonder why he doesn't look right, that is why.

All details require subtle shading and shaping to bring the piece to life. The best sources of information are magazines such as *Life* or *National Geographic*, which have clear color photos. Railroading magazines will show weathering on the trains themselves. Sharpen your sense of observation and look at colors and how light plays on various surfaces. Once you've mastered this, you'll be a true artist, capable of producing excellently detailed models.

Fig. 13-16 Hot-melt glue, putty, and a razor saw are all that you need to convert ordinary figures into exactly the right character for your layout.

Constructing and Modifying Ready-Mades

The most common figures are cast in plastic and have a built-in or glued-on base to keep them upright. The first step toward realism is to eliminate this base. If the base is only glued on, you can probably dissolve the glue joint with a few applications of liquid cement for plastics. Molded-on bases can be sawed off with a razor saw.

To support a figure, insert a nail or straight pin through its foot to fit into a corresponding hole on your layout. Use a No. 70 drill bit in a pin vise and drill a hole through one foot up into the leg. When the nail is in place, cut off the nail head with a pair of diagonal cutters, leaving $\frac{1}{8}$ to $\frac{1}{4}$ inch protruding from the figure. Drill a hole the same size in the layout where you want the figure to stand.

The procedures for painting or modifying figures is exactly like that of any other plastic model. Sand joints with 400-grit sandpaper and mold release lines with 600-grit sandpaper. Large dimples or holes can be filled using 3M spot putty. Follow the directions on the tube for filling or altering the figure.

Metal figures are trickier. Other than heft, there is little to recommend metal over plastic if the same figure is available in both materials. Most companies recommend using epoxy or super-glue for assembly, but both can cause problems. I prefer using hot-melt glue. The initial cost of the gun is higher, but it can be used economically for a variety of modeling and household jobs.

Painting Human Figures

Most model figures available today have incredible details, from their faces to their clothing, which is complete with tucks and folds. If not

Fig. 13-17 Figures are essential to adding life and scale reference to a diorama or layout. This figure is in $\frac{1}{25}$ scale for display with the MPC General. It has been primed with an airbrush and is ready for detail paint.

painted carefully, figures will lose their three-dimensional look. Shadow detail and highlights are an important part of painting figures.

The first step is to paint all the flesh areas. For a basic skin-tone color, mix one part Flesh PF23 and one part Reefer White PR11, using the Polly S brand of water-based paint. While the paint is still dry, use a size 000 brush or a brush with just two or three bristles and add shadows to the recessed areas around the eyes and neck. Folds and wrinkles are also just a shade darker. For this darker tone, mix one part Harvest Gold PF42 to nineteen parts water, and add four parts of dishwashing detergent per pint of paint. Dry-brush highlights on raised areas such as the cheekbones, forehead, and chin, as well as the backs of the fingers and wrists. For highlighting, mix one part Earth Yellow PF41, or one part Flesh PF23, or one part Mud PR83, to nine parts water, and add four parts of dishwashing detergent per pint of paint. Use a wash of brown to highlight the mouth.

Prepainted and Unpainted Animals

Domestic and farm animals are available prepainted in all scales from manufacturers such as AHM, Bachmann, LaBelle, Campbell/Weston, and Preiser. Unpainted animals are also available from some of the same manufacturers. The unpainted ones are best, since few of the prepainted animals look realistic. However, the painted figures easily can be further detailed to heighten the realism.

The first major change that needs to be made on prepainted animals is to spray them with a clear flat paint to kill the glossy finish. They can also benefit from dry-brushing a slightly darker shade of color over the figure to emphasize the hair texture. Barely touch the ends of the brush bristles to the paint and dab the model with very light strokes to produce hairlike streaks of color.

Photographing Model Layouts

Camera equipment can be puzzling, but, like anything else once you learn about it, there's no real mystery involved. The benefits of photography can be enjoyed almost immediately.

There is a fantastic array of camera equipment to choose from. Read some photography magazines and use common sense and you will select the right equipment for your purposes.

CHOOSING A CAMERA

Cameras range in price from simple box cameras that sell for just a few dollars to complex professional models selling for more than $1,000. Obviously, you want something between these two extremes.

The most popular camera on the market is the single-lens-reflex type, known as an SLR. This simply means that when you look through the viewfinder, you are looking right through the lens itself. Thus you always see exactly what the camera lens sees.

Whenever you see photographs where everybody has his head cut off, the picture was no doubt taken with an inexpensive range-finder camera. This is different from a single-lens-reflex camera because your eye sees something quite different from what the lens "sees" when you look through the viewfinder and press the shutter release, you may inadvertently cut so it sees the scene from a different angle. If you compose the picture in the viewfinder and press the shutter release, you may inadvertently cut off the top half of your subject.

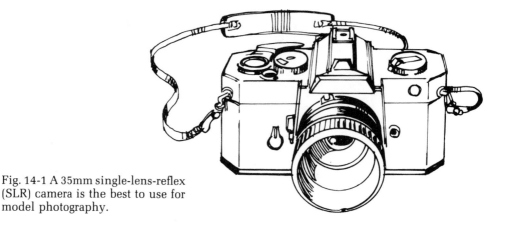

Fig. 14-1 A 35mm single-lens-reflex (SLR) camera is the best to use for model photography.

That won't happen with a single-lens-reflex camera, unless you're extremely careless. If you carefully compose the shot, you will see the same thing in the final picture. So for general purposes, an SLR is easier to use, although it's more expensive. But remember that a camera is a lifetime investment, which justifies the cost.

Single-lens-reflex cameras also take a variety of accessory lenses, which make the job of photographing different subjects easier. For instance, a wide-angle lens can be attached to the camera body after the standard lens has been removed. This allows you to photograph a wider area from the same viewpoint than you could with the standard lens. It's handy when shooting large background areas used as a backdrop for your main subject, and it has a good depth of field for image sharpness. If you want to shoot

Fig. 14-2 Range-finder cameras are ill-suited for model photography because of parallax problems.

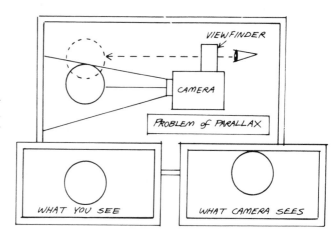

Fig. 14-3 Backlighting can completely wash out the subject.

a photo of something that is far away, you will need a telephoto lens (sometimes called a "long" lens).

A wide-angle and a telephoto lens will cover just about every photographic situation. Other than that, you'll need film, a talk with your local camera store operator, and practice.

Most single-lens-reflex cameras use 35mm film, which is inexpensive, so shoot a lot of it. Buy 36-exposure rolls so that you don't have to reload film so often. Try Kodak's excellent Tri-X black-and-white film, which practically allows you to shoot in the dark without a flash.

The Japanese have brought 35mm photography within nearly everyone's grasp with their mass-produced, high-quality cameras. Go to your camera store and have a salesperson help you. Pick up the cameras, handle them, ask questions. They all share lenses interchangeably, and they will usually feature as standard equipment a through-the-lens light meter, which allows correct exposure of the film according to how much light is available. Each camera operates a bit differently. Familiarize yourself with the

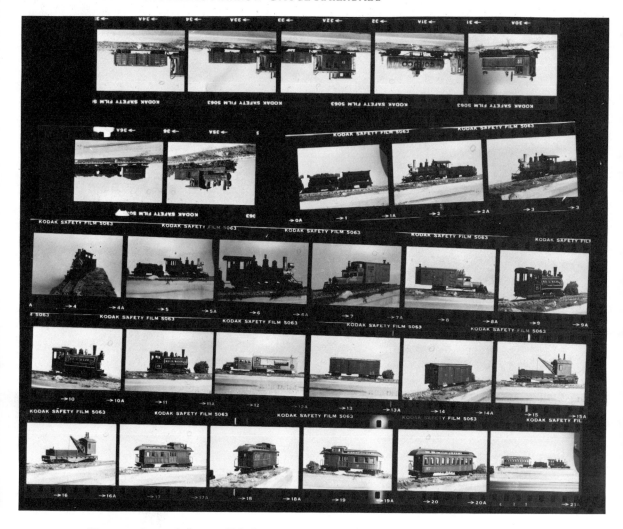

Fig. 14-4 A proof sheet will help you pick the best shots without going to the expense of having prints made of every shot.

camera you purchase. Read the instruction manual over and over, and handle the camera (without film in it) before you attempt a picture-taking session.

FILM PROCESSING

If you've shot, say, five rolls of 36-exposure film, that's 180 shots! Obviously you can't afford to have a black-and-white print made of each

Fig. 14-5 The depth of field in this photo is fairly good; it was shot at F-22.

one, even at cut-rate drugstore prices, let alone at a custom printer. Instead, take the film to a camera shop and ask for a proof or contact sheet for each roll. A proof sheet is actually a small black-and-white print of each shot. The prints are the same size as each frame of 35mm film. Professional photographers use these sheets to pick out only the best shots. Since all of the shots you take won't be sensational photos, use the proof sheet to pick out the best ones.

Of all the photos you take, there may be about a dozen that you will want to have made into prints. Simply mark "5×7" or "8×10" with a grease pencil across the frame on the proof sheet. Take the proof sheet and the negatives to a drugstore or camera store for custom printing.

Fig. 14-6 This photo was shot at F-2.8, and the entire background has been lost.

PHOTOGRAPHING MINIATURES

The biggest problem when photographing miniatures is depth of field. Consider this: A real train travels through mountains on a bright, clear day. With a standard short-focal-length lens (wide-angle and normal lenses), you should be able to capture the train, mountains, and sky all in focus. In order to re-create this in miniature, you must take special precautions to get proper depth. A limited depth of field always destroys the illusion of reality. The closer the object is to the camera, the less depth of field, so keep your distance. Wide-angle lenses have more apparent sharpness than telephoto lenses. A large F-stop (F/22 or 32) small aperture offers more depth of field than a small F-stop (F/1.8) large aperture.

Bibliography

Abdill, George B. *Pacific Slope Railroads.* Superior Publishing Company, Seattle, 1959.

Adams, Kramer. *Logging Railroads of the West.* Superior Publishing Company, Seattle, 1961.

Bender, Henry E. *Uintah Railway: The Gilsonite Route.* Howell-North Books, San Diego, 1968.

Best, Gerald M. *Nevada County Narrow Gauge.* Trans-Anglo Books, Corona del Mar, Calif., 1965.

———. *Railroads of Hawaii.* Golden West Books, San Marino, Calif., 1978.

———. *Ships and Narrow Gauge Rails: The Story of the Pacific Coast Company.* Howell-North Books, San Diego, 1964.

Carter, William. *Ghost Towns of the West.* Lane Publishing Company, Menlo Park, Calif., 1978.

Conde, Jesse C. *Sugar Trains Pictorial.* The Glenwood Collector's Series, 1975.

Cornwall, L. Peter, and Farrel, Jack W. *Ride the Sandy River.* Pacific Fast Mail, Edmunds, Wash., 1973.

Ferrell, Mallery Hope. *The Gilpin Gold Train.* Pruett Publishing Company, Boulder, Colo., 1970.

Fiedler, Mildred. *Railroads of the Black Hills.* Bonanza Books, New York, 1964.

Johnston, Hank. *Railroads of the Yosemite Valley.* Trans-Anglo Books, Corona del Mar, Calif., 1963.

Jones, Robert C. *Two Feet Between the Rails.* Sundance Publications, Silverton, Colo., 1979.

Koch, Michael. *The Shay Locomotive: Titan of the Timber.* The World Press, Denver, 1971.

Labbe, John T., and Goe, Vernon. *Railroads in the Woods.* Howell-North Books, San Diego, 1961.

MacGregor, Bruce H. *Narrow-Gauge Portrait, South Pacific Coast.* Glenwood Publishers, Felton, Calif., 1975.

Martin, Cy. *Gold Rush Narrow Gauge.* Trans-Anglo Books, Corona del Mar, Calif., 1974.

Moody, Linwood W. *The Maine Two-Footers.* Howell-North Books, San Diego, 1959.

Myrick, David F. *Railroads of Nevada and Eastern California.* Howell-North Books, San Diego, 1962.

Shaw, Frederic. *Little Railways of the World.* Howell-North Books, San Diego, 1958.

Small, Charles S. *Two-Foot Rails to the Front.* Railroad Monographs, 1982.

Turner, George. *Narrow-Gauge Nostalgia.* Trans-Anglo Books, Costa Mesa, Calif., 1971.

Whitehouse, Patrick, and Allen, Peter. *Narrow Gauge the World Over.* Ian Allen Ltd., London, 1976.

Wolf, Adolf H. *Rails in the Mother Lode.* Darwin Publications, Burbank, Calif., 1978.

Wurm, Ted, and Demoro, Harre. *The Silver Short Line.* Trans-Anglo Books, Glendale, Calif., 1983.

Index

Page numbers in **bold** type indicate illustrations.